Learning About the World: Reading Nonfiction

Lucy Calkins, Series Editor

Amanda Hartman

Photography by Peter Cunningham

Illustrations by Marjorie Martinelli

HEINEMANN ◆ PORTSMOUTH, NH

To Bernadette Fitzgerald, whose brilliant leadership of 503 has shown the world what is possible.

Heinemann
361 Hanover Street
Portsmouth, NH 03801–3912
www.heinemann.com

Offices and agents throughout the world

© 2015 by Amanda Hartman and Lucy Calkins

The authors and publisher wish to thank those who have generously given permission to reprint borrowed material:

Reprinted with permission from the book *Hang On, Monkey!* by Susan B. Neuman. © 2014 National Geographic Society.

From *Super Storms* © 2002 by Seymour Simon. Used by permission of Chronicle Books LLC, San Francisco. Visit ChronicleBooks.com

I Want To Be A Doctor, by Dan Liebman. Firefly Books, 2000. Used by permission of Firefly Books Ltd.

Owls, © 2012 by Capstone. All rights reserved.

Materials by Kaeden Books and Lee & Low Books, appearing throughout the primary Reading Units of Study series, are reproduced by generous permission of the publishers. A detailed list of credits is available in the Grade 1 online resources.

Cataloging-in-Publication data is on file with the Library of Congress.

ISBN-13: 978-0-325-07704-8

Series editorial team: Anna Gratz Cockerille, Karen Kawaguchi, Tracy Wells, Felicia O'Brien, Debra Doorack, Jean Lawler, Marielle Palombo, and Sue Paro
Production: Elizabeth Valway, David Stirling, and Abigail Heim
Cover and interior designs: Jenny Jensen Greenleaf
Photography: Peter Cunningham
Illustrations: Marjorie Martinelli
Composition: Publishers' Design and Production Services, Inc.
Manufacturing: Steve Bernier

Printed in the United States of America on acid-free paper
19 18 17 16 15   EBM   2 3 4 5

Acknowledgments

THE PAGES OF THIS BOOK brim with the ideas the Teachers College Reading and Writing Project (TCRWP) has developed over years—decades, really. The ideas we develop in our think tanks and research projects are here, the ideas we share in summer institutes are here, and most of all, the ideas that come to life in reading workshop classrooms throughout the world are here. It's great fun to read through the pages, whispering small thank yous for insights, methods, ideas, stories.

I want to thank Lucy Calkins for giving me the opportunity to write this book—and for her mentorship in teaching me not just how to teach well, but how to write well. Lucy, all of the ideas and insights that make up this book are a direct result of the work that you lead at the TCRWP. Thank you for all the think tanks, workshops, Thursday study groups, conversations and debates, and for your help writing this book.

Abby Heim, thank you for being the guiding light throughout this project. Your tireless support and direction have meant so much to me. Anna Gratz Cockerille, your leadership, too, has been invaluable. The energy that you both give to writers is precious, and I thank you.

A big thanks to the editors, Marielle Palombo and Beth Moore, for the ever important work of sharpening and clarifying parts to ensure a coherent whole. Thank you for your attention to detail and for pushing this book to be as clear and concise as possible.

And, oh, how I want to thank my community at TCRWP. Thank you, colleagues, for all the ideas that you share, for being ever willing to try things out with teachers and kids and to come back to the drawing board to revise, rethink, and extend. Thank you for your relentless effort to build knowledge together and to bring that knowledge to schools throughout the country and the world. I want to thank the leadership at the project: Laurie Pessah, Kathleen Tolan, Mary Ehrenworth, and, of course, Lucy. I want to thank reading specialist Cheryl Tyler and the terrific team of primary staff developers: Shanna Schwartz, Christine Holley, Natalie Louis, Lauren Kolbeck, Monique Knight, Celena Larkey, Rebecca Cronin, Lindsay Mann, Lindsay Wilkes, Lindsay Barton, Rachel Rothman, Katie Wears, Marjorie Martinelli, Brianna Parlitsis, Allyse Bader, April Delude, Jennifer DeSutter, Valerie Geschwind, Bianca Lavey, Marie Mounteer, Angela Baez, and Dani Sturtz.

I would also like to recognize and thank Rebecca Rappaport Sanghvi, Julie Steinberg, Beth Moore, and Nilaja Taylor who generously gave their wisdom and time to this book. I'd also like to give a special thank you to Julia Mooney and Elizabeth Dunford Franco for not only all their contributions to this book but also for all the collaboration throughout the years, imagining and writing together. Thank you.

I certainly couldn't have done this work without the collaboration of administrators, teachers, and, of course, children. In particular, I would like to thank Kathy Moore in San Ramon Unified District in California, Adele Schroeder at 59M, Anthony Inzerillo at 199Q, Bernadette Fitzgerald at 503BK, and Liz Phillips at 321BK.

Lastly, I want to thank my family and friends for all their support this past year in helping me to keep moving forward. Thank you for your patience, understanding, and everlasting belief in this work.

—Amanda

Contents

BEND III   Reading Aloud Like Experts

Read-Aloud and Shared Reading

An Orientation to the Unit

IF THERE IS ONE DEFINING characteristic of the young child, it is curiosity. Think of a youngster on the morning after a rain storm, out on your driveway or your sidewalk. Chances are good that child will be crouching alongside one of the worms that has washed up in the rain. Peering at the worm, the child will ask, "Why did he come out? Where is his mouth? Where is his behind?" The questions are incessant, and they last all day. At breakfast, the child asks, "How do they get the seeds out of grapes with no seeds?" Then, looking up at the sky, "Where does the moon go in the day?"

At the start of this unit, you'll build on that natural curiosity by telling your children, "We're going to learn about the world. We're going to swim with sharks. We're going to travel back in time. We'll hold baby monkeys and crystals in our hands! Who knows? Maybe we'll even go on adventures to the moon and to the planets in outer space." When the kids wonder how that can be true, you'll unveil a section of your classroom library, previously shrouded in a sheet. "Books can help us learn about the world!"

This unit on nonfiction reading comes early in the year because it is important for children to know, right from the start, that books can teach them about submarines and thunder, dinosaurs, and iPads. By devoting a unit of study to nonfiction reading, you put yourself on the front edge of primary literacy instruction in this country. Studies of first-grade classrooms have shown that students spend an average of only 3.6 minutes each day interacting with information texts—less in low socioeconomic status schools (Duke 2000). You'll be departing from that in a gigantic way, and in time, the world will follow your lead. The Common Core State Standards and other world-class standards suggest that there should be a 50/50 division between fiction and nonfiction across the whole day, across all grades. Whether your district adheres to those standards or not, their guidance on this front is solid. Think of how much of your reading is nonfiction: train schedules, restaurant reviews,

websites, newspapers, blogs, professional books, memos, and biographies. Think of how much children need to learn about the world—even to understand just one thing, say, clouds—in order to construct concepts about a host of related topics: weather, rain, the water cycle, evaporation, gravity, forms of water, air, and forecasting. All that, just to mull over their questions about the gray clouds rolling in overhead.

The excitement you're drumming up will fuel the hard work your students will be doing across the unit as they read nonfiction books to learn, learn, learn. It's early in first grade and your children have a lot of growing to do as readers of any text, not just nonfiction texts, so the unit balances support for nonfiction reading with support for reading processes. Children think of the first bend of the unit as being all about how nonfiction readers become super smart about topics, but teachers know that as they rally children to learn all that they can from their books, they are also teaching comprehension strategies, such as previewing the text, predicting, noticing text structure, and synthesizing information from multiple sources (the picture, the print, the text boxes).

The second bend continues the emphasis on comprehension and basic reading processes, but puts a spotlight on vocabulary. This bend helps readers develop good habits for decoding unfamiliar words and for working to understand new vocabulary. It's critical that students incorporate the domain-specific words they encounter into their talk, and you'll support them in using all the important words they learn in conversations with their partners.

In the final bend, you'll shift your emphasis to building fluency and studying craft, teaching students how to revisit texts to reread in smoother voices, to sound like experts, and to notice craft moves authors make that they also can make and discuss. The unit culminates with students planning and sharing their own read-alouds with others, orchestrating all they have learned in order to give someone else the gift of knowledge.

THE INTERSECTION OF READING DEVELOPMENT AND THIS UNIT

This year in your first-graders' lives is one marked by tremendous reading growth. Your students will soar through reading levels this year more than any other. You'll marvel at students who enter the year as beginner readers, just starting to "break the code" in reading, who will skip out the door in June, having blossomed into proficient readers. You'll watch as they word solve with increased ease and flexibility, select books that feed their interests, and grow ideas through studying the pictures and words on the page with others.

First-graders enter this unit having just immersed themselves in the habits and behaviors that make for powerful reading. In Unit 1, *Readers Build Good Habits*, you built off the work students did at the end of kindergarten, when they became avid readers, making reading playdates and learning to sustain reading even when the world threatened to distract them. In your first unit this year, you supported students in learning new habits and strategies that will propel them forward as readers, and it's critical that you maintain that strong work within this unit. Just because students have a new bag of books and are in a new unit, it doesn't mean they can let go of their earlier learning. During this unit, make sure your students continue to read a high volume of books and use their reading mats to keep track of that reading. Remind them of the strategies they know for solving tricky words, and coach them to use those strategies as needed.

Just as your students may linger with questions, you will want to help them linger to study a page of a book. Often times in reading, much like in writing workshop, students at this age are eager to read and write the words as quickly as they can and to be done! They have grown just enough muscle and strength in their knowledge of spelling and phonics that they can zip through their books quickly. Helping them to slow down will help them learn more information about their topics and it will help them infer more as well. Often times, the information books for these beginner readers (levels E–G) hold more information in the pictures than in the words, so at this stage in reading, you will want to show students how they can do the work of connecting the information in the words with the information in the pictures.

In this unit, you'll ask kids to think about how they learn information from words and also from illustrations, especially from photographs. You'll teach them to ask, "What's happening in this picture?" and to imagine what happened before or after the photograph was taken. When your students were a bit less experienced as readers, they looked to the pictures for help producing the words that the picture represented. But by now, they are ready to see more in those static images. Imagine your students saying things like, "She's probably going to swing her other leg, the tree's probably shaking. The baby monkey is holding on to his mother so he doesn't fall."

First-graders need to make extraordinary progress over the course of this year. Many first-grade readers move from level D all the way to level J in one year. These levels were designed to help readers to move! Between levels D and J, students' most important work will revolve around integrating sources of information and developing flexibility in solving words on the run. As your kids begin reading level G books, you will be looking for them to start fixing up their reading at, or at least very close to, the point of error. You also want to see that students are using all three sources of information—meaning, structure, and visual (MSV)—to not just attempt words but also to fix them when something is not quite right. Supporting this will be front and center in your mind for your first-graders because without your guidance, first-graders aren't great at self-correcting. They *do* begin to internalize a sense of right and wrong and to worry—so harness their worries over "not doing it right" and turn that energy into an instinct to self-correct.

As readers progress towards levels F/G, you'll see that even readers who are well on track begin to have different strengths and weaknesses. For example, one reader might be great at using word substitutions but doesn't really ever break words into parts or look back to see if what she read looks right. On the other hand, another reader breaks words into parts but never checks in to be sure that what she is reading is actually a word. In both cases, you want to bolster the other sources of information to help the student work more flexibly and to become stronger at using phonics knowledge to solve words, using meaning all the while.

At these levels, many of your students are working on using parts of words (usually CVC patterns) at the beginning of words, looking for little words inside of bigger words, breaking longer words into parts, and using inflectional endings such as *ing*. You will want to support their energy and enthusiasm for this work. As their books become more complex, words will become longer and your readers will need stamina for working through the hard parts of reading.

As the unit progresses, you will want to support your readers to grow not only in their ability to word solve but also in their knowledge of vocabulary. Because the topics that students will be reading about will tend to be roughly familiar ones, the vocabulary should feel within grasp. However, your children will be reading books now that may contain words they don't know—even after a child reads *pennant*, for example, the child may not know what it means. Nonfiction books at the levels covered at this time of year often clearly define vocabulary words or make it easy for the reader to get the meaning from illustrations or "call outs." You'll want to teach readers to build meaning from these sources. Your first-graders will love for you to encourage them to try to use the book words in their social language. And using the words that children see in books is a big deal.

As readers, your children transition from pointing under words with their fingers to using their eyes to "scoop up" more words at a time, reading in longer, meaningful phrases. If a child is reading in a word-by-word way, you'll coach that child to stop at the end of the sentence or page and reread, putting more words together at a time to read in a voice much like talking. You may teach a small group of students to notice words such as *in*, *of*, *with*, and *to* and to use these words as a signal that they will need to read the next few words in a group (scoop them up). You may coach readers to read beginning phrases like "In the morning" as a group.

Many of your young readers are fans of nature shows on television, like *Wild Kratts*. Showing students short clips of how these scientists use their voice to sound interesting and important will help them think about how they can add teacher-like expression when they are rereading out loud to partners.

This unit also supports your children's social growth. Being the big kid is important to most of your students. They're no longer the littlest kids in the building, and in this unit they have a chance to mentor the youngest students. In kindergarten, they played teacher with their partners, and now they have a slightly more public opportunity to teach and share what they know. Nonfiction, with its implied invitation to become an expert and share knowledge, is a genre ideally suited for this invitation. At the end of this unit, we suggest you invite a kindergarten class in so your first graders can read to them. Such an invitation will help build confident, self-reliant readers.

OVERVIEW

Bend I: Getting Smart on Nonfiction Topics

As children learn to read, over and over you will encourage them to integrate knowledge from multiple sources—from print, syntax, and meaning. And over and over, you will see them ignore one of those sources of knowledge to grip onto another. Often, they ignore comprehension, forgetting to think about the text and about what would make sense in a sentence, and they do this to get both hands around the sequence of letters in a tricky word. The problem is that even decoding the words alone requires the youngster to draw on the very thing the child has ignored: meaning.

At the start of this unit, you will take a fresh approach towards supporting kids' proficiency with the reading process. You will support the tricky, multidimensional work of integrating sources—the work that is at the heart of what first-graders need to learn to do. In kid language, you teach kids to squeeze all the knowledge they can out of the books they are reading.

Research shows that equipping youngsters with a few comprehension strategies makes a big difference. To teach those strategies, you will model them, often utilizing a book that will weave through a big portion of your unit. *Hang on, Monkey!* by Susan Neuman is a book probably at the reading level of most students in your class. Research shows that even a small amount of explicit instruction in comprehension strategies increases children's comprehension dramatically, especially when that instruction teaches kids what the strategy is, when to use it, how to use it, and why to use it (National Reading Panel 2000; Pressley 2000)—all of which you'll do.

Instead of just looking at the monkey hanging by its arm from the tree, you may demonstrate how you preview by studying the picture, saying, "I've always thought they used their *tails* to hang, but this monkey is using its *arm*! Are you thinking more about this part as well? Fascinating." Not only will you support children in setting themselves up to read nonfiction texts, but you'll also remind students that they need to do something as readers at the end of a book, just as they learned in the previous unit.

Later, you might draw your finger to different parts of the same text and talk about what you notice in each part—thereby giving kids a concrete strategy to use in order to be similarly observant and thoughtful. You will also voice over as you demonstrate a strategy. You might say to your children, "Readers, did you notice that in order to learn a lot from even just that one page, we didn't just let the pages fly by? Instead, we thought, 'This *one page* can make us smarter,' and we read that page closely, with fingers and eyes moving across the page, thinking about what we saw, and getting as much out of it as we could."

Let's be clear about what you need to make happen in your classroom. Children must be given the opportunity to read a lot of nonfiction books, and they must be taught strategies for reading them. If not they will be flipping through the books to locate weird animal snouts or naked butts and not reading words at all, or they will be robotically churning through the sentences, tackling the hard words, without displaying a lot of curiosity about the topic.

In the first bend of the unit, you will teach strategies not just for thinking about the pictures and integrating that knowledge into work with words, but also for thinking about the sentences. Of course, children can't think for ten minutes about each picture and each sentence, but you do want to teach them what it really means to "think about the text." You'll want to help them know that readers often pause to envision what they are reading, making a picture of what they have read or adding what they learn from the words onto what they see in the existing picture.

Your teaching will support and extend the partner work you began in Unit 1. You'll do this by rallying partners to be "Super Helpers," holding one another accountable for planning what books they will read and how they will read them. You teach readers that it pays off to hold in-the-mind-only chats about what they're learning while reading and that then, when they have been reading for a while and get a chance to actually chat with a partner, those chats can be times to look back on books and recall what they learned and to think about that content. You may demonstrate how you would chat to yourself (which, remember, really means thinking to yourself) about one page, and then invite students to compare the way they were chatting with themselves with what they saw you do. "See how I thought about the pictures *and* the words, and I thought about what happened before and what might happen next? I had a little chat in my mind about this page. Was your chat the same as mine, or did it go differently?"

You will also want to provide additional models of what these conversations look like. To do this, you might gather students around a partnership in a fishbowl, highlighting the beautiful moves they make and that you want

everyone to note. You can voice over key moves you want students to pay attention to. "Cool! They are reading the words *and* looking at the pictures." Later you might add, "Oh, it looks like they're about to chat about what they are thinking. Let's listen and give a thumbs up if they do something terrific you could do, too." In these ways, your teaching will support readers in thinking and talking about the information they are learning, not just regurgitating a few facts or brushing past new information.

The unit suggests that you wrap up the bend with a fitting celebration designed to support students in sharing all their new learning with others—perhaps with a pretend tea party or pizza party. If you choose that option, you'll tell your kids, "When grown-ups are at parties (like the tea party we're having), they don't just eat! They also talk—and often they talk about the books they've been reading and the fun new things they're learning. Today, let's have fun talking about books, just like grown-ups do, by sharing important information and interesting ideas and asking questions about our books." You might go a step farther and dramatize a conversation to give students a sense of how it might go.

Bend II: Tackling Super Hard Words in Order to Keep Learning

In the second bend, you'll build on the strategies students learned in the first unit for solving hard words. This is critical work. As your readers begin to move into levels F/G/H and beyond, they will encounter increasingly complex, multisyllabic words in their texts. Some of these will be words that require decoding but that once children pronounce the word, they'll realize what it says and means. But other words will be unfamiliar to your children even after they can say them. Even once the child can pronounce the word, the meaning doesn't dawn on the child because the word is totally unfamiliar. This will pose a challenge that most of your first-graders haven't faced prior to now.

Because this is challenging work, we suggest you issue a rallying cry. You'll acknowledge that, yes, the words they're tackling will present big obstacles, and you'll tell students that tackling those obstacles will be a ton of fun, like tackling the tough challenges in an obstacle course. You may say, "Imagine it's like climbing up that big mountain of tires! It feels hard at first, but it feels great once you've done it!" Then, you might dramatize this work for students, first showing what not to do when they face a tricky word—slumping in the seat, tossing the book aside dismissively—and then demonstrating how readers can instead rise to the challenge of a tricky word. In this way, you'll be teaching an effort-based view of learning, conveying to children that it is a great privilege to be able to work with tenacity on work that matters.

Too often when students approach a tricky word, they look only at one part, perhaps at the initial sound, or read through individual phonemes and then wait until the end of the word to try to blend the sounds together. Even when these strategies work, they are inefficient, and your teaching here will support students in using the sources of information and their current word-solving strategies *better*. You'll want to help them to read words part by part, crashing those parts together—and what six-year-old won't be excited about crashing things!—by moving from the beginning part of the word, through the whole word, putting each part together again from the beginning. For example, you might take the word *forests* and demonstrate for students how you start with /for/, then read the next part and blend it together with the first: /for/ + /est/ = forest. "Forest! Is *forest* a word I know? Yes! Does is look right? Wait, there is another letter: forest+/s/= forests!" you might say and invite students to join you in rereading the whole sentence to make sure it makes sense and sounds right as well.

Remember that whenever a spotlight is placed on decoding words, first-graders can focus single-mindedly on how to say a word, losing sight of what the word itself means. Since many of the tricky words in nonfiction texts are important, domain-specific words, just sounding them out and moving on would be totally insufficient. Instead, you might say, "It's important to be on the lookout for *keywords*, words that are key to understanding your topic. It's like these words unlock knowledge." Gesture turning a key to help students visualize the work keywords do in nonfiction texts. "When you find a keyword, try extra hard not to just read that word and say that word, but to own that word." You'll teach readers that when they run into a new word, they say it the best they can and then think, "What does this new word mean?" Coach them to use the pictures, the words, and what they know about the topic to figure out the word's meaning.

Of course, students will encounter familiar words that are important to the topic, and you'll want to teach them to incorporate all the important words they encounter into conversations about their topics. Connecting this to your readers' lives will help. You might say, "Each one of you is already an expert on things you know from your life. Is there someone here who is an expert on soccer? Stand up and take a bow." Once the giggles and bows subside, you'll say, "I'm pretty sure you know a whole BUNCH of soccer words, am I right?" Marvel as kids list all the soccer words they know, and then teach them that the work of getting to know keywords related to a topic and using them is work experts on any topic do.

One day, you'll invite students to play a guessing game with the new words they have been collecting, describing each word with clues and examples so a partner can accurately guess what the word is. "It's part of an elephant's body," you might hint, "and it's long, wrinkled, and gray. Elephants use it like an arm. What word is it?" This not only draws students' attention to important keywords in the text, it also helps them create a context for talking about these words.

In Bend III, you'll add some instruction to get students to read nonfiction texts with a bit more emphasis and proper intonation. To get kids ready for this, you might begin coaching them to think about the sound of their reading voices, particularly when they reread. You'll show students how their voices can reflect more meaning and provide emphasis to help convey what a word, phrase, or whole section means. To do this, you could show students a short video clip of a nonfiction topic, perhaps a clip from *Wild Kratts*, a PBS nature show, and then say, "This is not just a fun show to watch. It's a show that teaches people a lot about the world! Watching a show like this is similar to reading books. When you are reading, try to make your voice sound like the voices in a show like this one." Then, you'll coach students to use their voices to add emphasis, or, in kid language, "punch out" some words. Working on phrasing and stress, key aspects of fluency, can help students progress as readers, particularly at these earlier levels, and improves not just word solving and fluency but also students' comprehension. Your teaching in Bend III will extend this work.

Bend III: Reading Aloud Like Experts

In the third and final bend of the unit, you'll invite students to give a gift of knowledge to others by planning their own nonfiction read-alouds for an audience of kindergartners, and you'll help them plan those read-alouds by showing them how you plan your read-alouds. You will encourage your students to gather a small stack of familiar books, and to read and reread those books until they can practically perform them. Across the bend, you'll support students in reading their chosen books like gold, using their voices to show the big feelings of each part and to highlight the keywords. And you'll teach them that just as teachers pause during a read-aloud to think aloud or to invite listeners to talk and think, they will also need to pause to think aloud and to ask questions.

We find that getting students to read aloud to others with purpose and energy boosts their investment in the work and is one of the best ways to rally children to reread, thus supporting fluency development. Inviting students to take on the teacher role supports student talk and comprehension. Many children enjoy playing the part of the teacher, and you'll find they can mimic your moves quite well, adapting the highly charged, full-of-energy kind of talk you model in your read-alouds.

You'll highlight various ways to reread texts and do this in ways that places a special emphasis on reading like a writer, noticing the fabulous craft moves an author has used and then using what they notice to read selected pages in ways that pop out the craft moves so listeners appreciate them as well. You may draw their attention to text structure, knowing a focus on structure can support students with prediction, monitoring for meaning, and determining importance. Students will notice that some books are organized as "All About" texts, whereas others include stories. You'll teach students that readers can study pages in their texts thinking, "What did this author do here that I could try?" and then they can highlight those moves in their read-alouds.

With every great read-aloud, there is always a bit of drama. Drama is nothing new to your first-graders. In fact, studies estimate that 93% of the meaning we derive from oral communication is perceived through facial expressions, gestures, and tone of voice. Think about what this means for reading aloud to children! You might say to your students, "When I watch you pretending and dramatizing, I see you using your body. Using your body during reading means making gestures, actions, or expressions that help explain information in the book." Then, you might invite students to try this work with you, pulling out a line from a text, perhaps "Owls gulp small prey in one bite," and using their bodies to show what that line really *looks* like.

You'll bring the unit to a close by inviting a kindergarten class in to celebrate all your students have learned. "First-graders, you are in charge! You will be reading and helping your newest reading buddies listen, think, and talk with you!" Watch and listen in amazement, celebrating the dramatic growth you see in your youngsters.

ASSESSMENT

Conduct running records, both formal and informal ones.

It is important to continue to assess how your students are using the reading process and what their strengths and needs are. First, you will want to continue to use your running records to help you think about reading process and how your students are using and integrating the sources of information as they read. You will also want to note both how their fluency is progressing and how well they understand what they read.

As your readers continue to grow and change, fluency will play an increasingly important role. As emergent and beginning readers, it was necessary for your children to point crisply to one word at a time, often reading in a choppy, staccato fashion until the book became more familiar on subsequent rereads. As kids move into levels F, G, and beyond, you can begin teaching children to read with greater fluency. Take notes in the margins of your running records forms:

- Does the child still point under words?

- Does the child pause often to solve many words, with little or no automaticity?

- Does the child read only one or two words at a time, rarely scooping words into meaningful phrases?

Beginning at level J, the TCRWP running records include a fluency scale that helps you determine if the child's fluency on a first read indicates that the level is a good match for that reader. In general, once children are reading at about level J, even the first read should include these hallmarks of strong fluency (Rasinski): accuracy, automaticity, parsing (or reading in phrases), and prosody (or expression). Reading should sound natural and expressive, with appropriate reading rate and overall tone—if not, the level may be too challenging.

At this point in the year, late fall/early winter, you should expect your readers to be approaching levels F and G in order to achieve the end-of-year benchmark. You will probably need to take running records to determine their progress. If you have a system for doing this with nonfiction texts, that's great, but if you don't, then either use leveled books or take running records of children's reading of narratives. Analyzing (formal or informal) running records will give you insight into the strategies your students rely on for decoding, fluency, and comprehension as well as help you keep track of their progress up the gradient of book difficulty. Doing a miscue analysis to determine how children are integrating sources of information (meaning, syntax, and visual) will also help you make decisions about what print work to teach each of your readers next. When you find that a student draws solely on visual information, decoding words letter by letter, and does not search meaning to decode or understand the word, it is often the case that she will do the same when encountering unknown words in nonfiction books. You'll want to help such students set a goal to cross-check what they say and ask themselves, "Does that make sense? Do I know a word that sounds similar that would match the information in the book?" This is an important goal in reading, regardless of the genre.

Assess students' thinking in nonfiction books.

As you gear up for this unit, you'll first want to find out what your readers already know about reading nonfiction. You might do an informal assessment during a read-aloud, selecting key points in an engaging high-interest text (one that is at grade level text complexity) at which to pause and ask children to talk to one another. You can match your prompts to the key strategies and skills highlighted in this unit (main ideas, or word solving and vocabulary, for example). For example, in Bend I, you will be emphasizing learning main ideas, so in your read-aloud assessment, after reading an especially detailed short section, you might prompt students to tell their partner what they think that section was *mostly* about. As children talk to one another, circulate around the room, making notes of their responses. You might be surprised at how difficult it can be for some children to synthesize and summarize. Do some children list lots of tiny details, with nothing to connect them? Do any

children revert to discussing a connection they have to a personal experience with little information from the actual text? As children talk, you can quickly ascertain who in your class will need support with discussing main ideas from the information in their nonfiction books.

Perhaps instead you'll prompt children to figure out the meaning of key vocabulary since this is major work in the second bend. You might stop at several words that are likely to be unfamiliar, and ask children to draw a picture representing what they think the word might mean or to choose from three pictures the one that best matches the meaning. Then you can collect those pictures and quickly sort into rough groupings—children that had no difficulty figuring out the meaning of new vocabulary, children who showed some signs of understanding new vocabulary, and children who will clearly need lots of support with vocabulary.

As the unit unfolds, you might also do some assessment during conferring to see what children do when asked to discuss nonfiction books. Throughout the unit, you can check in with students using the books they are reading, or familiar read-alouds, asking questions such as "Hmm, we learned so many facts in this section, didn't we? What do you think was the main thing that all those fact had in common? How does all the information fit together in this book?" As you conduct this research as part of your regular conferring, you can jot notes that will help inform your teaching.

Consider other assessments to track student growth and set instructional goals.

You may want to re-administer the high-frequency-word assessment if your students have mastered the words from your initial assessment at the start of the year to find what new words to tackle next in word study and word wall work with your students. Chances are there will be groups of students who need different words to work on. To differentiate, you may add to your students' individual word rings that they have developed from Unit 1.

If your students have moved several levels as readers, or if you take a look at students' current independent writing, and it seems likely that your students have moved into new stages as spellers since the first assessment, then you may want to administer another spelling inventory to know which features of phonics to work on next. You will see that your students have grown as spellers and will be able to use more features as readers. Particularly at levels F, G, and H, students are using inflectional endings, becoming more aware of long vowels in words, and breaking words into parts instead of looking letter-by-letter.

If you have students well below benchmark, you may find that they need instruction in very different features of phonics and possibly have a shortage of high-frequency words. You also may have some very beginner readers that still need support with learning all their letter names and sounds. If your students are new to you, and did not come with a folder of assessments from their previous school, you may want to give letter/sound identification assessments now.

You can refer to the assessment and word study chapters in *A Guide to the Reading Workshop, Primary Grades*, for a complete picture of all the assessments you might select, including where to find these assessments and how to administer them.

Use your assessment data to tailor your curriculum to the needs of your students.

The data that you collected at the end of Unit 1 and the information you gather at the very start of this unit can help inform your decisions. Will you dive into this unit? Or will you teach an alternate unit first? Will you teach this unit as is? Or will you add a bend or two, or supplement this unit with another write-up?

For the most part, you will probably want to move from Unit 1 right into Unit 2. The support that this book provides will cover a broad range of needs. As you head into this unit, you may want to look to *If . . . Then . . . Curriculum: Assessment-Based Instruction, Grades K–2*, as a resource for extra practice with the skills introduced in this unit. You might use the alternate unit of study, "Growing Expertise in Little Books: Nonfiction Reading," as a supplement to this unit, teaching the content from that unit to a group (or groups) of your students (those that you know will need extra support with vocabulary, especially). Or, you might decide to use particular bends from the alternate unit to extend the work of this unit, giving your whole class a little extra practice with particular skills. Should you decide to insert an extra bend, you will want to be mindful about pacing; know that six weeks is about the right amount of time to spend in a given unit. After that, student engagement will wane, and their growth may plateau.

However, it is possible, at the start of first grade that your classroom may be filled with readers who are reading well below the benchmark. This may be particularly true if your students did not have reading workshop consistently in the past, or did not build up the stamina or volume to grow into their potential as readers. You might find it necessary to insert a unit on foundational skills before diving into a unit on nonfiction reading. If you look across your assessments and discover that many of your first-graders are still reading at levels C/D/E and are in need of support with emergent and beginning print strategies after the first unit of study, then you may want to look to *If . . . Then . . . Curriculum: Assessment-Based Instruction, Grades K–2*, as a resource. You may want to teach the alternate unit "Readers Are Resourceful: Tackling Hard Words and Tricky Parts in Books" before diving into this unit).

Another consideration is for first-graders who are mostly reading at the benchmark levels for early-mid first grade (levels E/F/G) but clearly need additional support with print strategies. If you find that many of your students skip words or give up very easily when they encounter unfamiliar vocabulary, then you might want to teach the unit "Word Detectives Use All They Know to Solve Words" from the *If . . . Then . . .* book before this unit of study. This unit is similar to "Readers Are Resourceful: Tackling Hard Words and Tricky Parts in Books," but it is geared for readers reading levels E/F/G, so be sure to preview the units and select the one that best matches your students' needs.

GETTING READY

Gather a variety of high-interest informational books that span your students' current just-right levels.

For this unit, you will want your students to be able to access just-right nonfiction books from your classroom library. If you have students reading between levels E and J, be sure to have plenty of texts at those levels, ideally for students to be able to select 10–12 books a week. You may decide to reorganize your leveled library into separate baskets of nonfiction books at each level, and you may decide to cover the shelves of baskets with a sheet and then unveil them with kids when you launch the unit. This will help to draw out the excitement, as well as make it easier to shop for the books that they will need for reading.

You may find that you do not yet have enough nonfiction books in your library at each level. Do not fret. There are several things that you can do. First, instead of having students collect their own set of nonfiction books, students can share between 10 and 12 books out of a bin of just-right nonfiction books. Your school may have a book closet, from which classrooms share nonfiction books, or a cart that rolls from classroom to classroom with bins of nonfiction books to read. There are several structures that you could invent so that you are able to get just-right nonfiction books into the hands of your readers.

Collect texts you'll use for minilessons and guided reading.

You'll want to gather informational texts that you can use for minilessons, along with guided reading sets that are slightly above your students' independent reading levels. In your read-aloud and shared reading, you will probably use some texts that are close to the just-right book levels that your students are reading. This would mean, in the late fall/early winter, if your students are reading on benchmark, you will want to choose a text somewhere between level E and level G. You will also want to make sure that the texts you select have inviting photographs, where students can learn and find even more information. *Hang On, Monkey!* by Susan B. Neuman and *I Want to Be a Doctor* by Dan Liebman are two texts that will grab the attention of your students and help them become not only knowledgeable but also more strategic.

You may want to also gather a few videos so that you can show informational texts in other forms. Students can interact with these videos as they do with books. You might use something like a short scene from *Wild Kratts* on PBS, which is a nature show narrated by two biologist brothers, showing kids how to be fascinated about the world. Watching informational videos can help students imagine the voice they can practice using as they read, both in their head and out loud.

READ-ALOUD AND SHARED READING

Select books that have complex stories that are engaging and will be fun to talk and think about.

For your read-aloud work in this unit, you will want to select books that are not only at a variety of reading levels but also have engaging information that will spark deeper conversations. At the back of this book, you will find a section that has a three-day plan written out for using *Super Storms* by Seymour Simon (level L). This book has both captivating photographs and interesting information that spark great conversations and ideas. Seymour Simon writes about various types of super storms and what makes them dangerous. He describes the damages and dangers as well as some of the precautions that people take to protect themselves.

This text will be complicated, which will push even your highest readers to think more deeply, learn new words, and think about how keywords relate to the subject. You will want to choose other engaging books, about topics that will draw your students' attention and enthusiasm, as well as texts that will provoke good book talk.

Use the read-aloud plan at the back of this book to prepare for one read-aloud across a couple of days as well as others across the unit.

The three-day plan will give you listening prompts, turn-and-talk prompts, and think-aloud prompts to use throughout *Super Storms*. Not only will this plan give you the skills and strategies to practice, but you can take these yellow Post-it notes and use them again and again throughout the unit, across the variety of texts that you select to read. You will find that these skills are transferable and echo the work that is happening in your minilessons, conferences, and small-group work.

Select books that will teach the main skills that echo your unit of study and what your students need as readers.

For your shared reading, you may decide to read *Owls* by Mary Dunn (level H). This is a book that teaches the reader all about owls: the way they move, the ways owls look, the way they hunt, and the way baby owls grow up. This book also has amazing close-up photographs to study as well as interesting information and vocabulary to learn and think more about.

Use the five-day plan, in the back of this book, to help you prepare for shared reading.

After the read-aloud section in this book is a section on shared reading. Here you will find a five-day plan for shared reading, with the text *Owls* as an example of how to weave in the foundational skills needed in this unit. These plans are to be taught alongside the unit, echoing the teaching and supporting your reads to move up the trajectory of reading and thinking in more complex texts. These plans are meant to be replicable, so that for the remaining weeks of the unit you can repeat the plan with other texts. To learn more about read-aloud and shared reading go to Chapters 12 and 13 in *A Guide to the Reading Workshop, Primary Grades*.

✳ ONLINE DIGITAL RESOURCES

A variety of resources to accompany this and the other Grade 1 Units of Study for Teaching Reading are available in the Online Resources, including charts and examples of student work shown throughout *Learning About the World*, as well as links to other electronic resources. Offering daily support for your teaching, these materials will help you provide a structured learning environment that fosters independence and self-direction.

To access and download all the digital resources for the Grade 1 Units of Study for Teaching Reading:

1. Go to **www.heinemann.com** and click the link in the upper right to log in. (If you do not have an account yet, you will need to create one.)

2. **Enter the following registration code** in the box to register your product: RUOS_Gr1

3. Under **My Online Resources**, click the link for the ***Grade 1 Reading Units of Study***.

4. The digital resources are available in the upper right; click a file name to download. (For any compressed ("ZIP") files, double-click the downloaded file to extract individual files to your hard drive.)

(You may keep copies of these resources on up to six of your own computers or devices. By downloading the files you acknowledge that they are for your individual or classroom use and that neither the resources nor the product code will be distributed or shared.)

Getting Started as a Nonfiction Reader

IN THIS SESSION, you'll remind students what they already know about sneak peeks and teach them how that knowledge will help them as readers learning about new topics.

GETTING READY

✔ Organize your library so that students have baskets of leveled nonfiction books available for them to self-select texts. Before the lesson, have students choose just-right books to fill their book baggies with a mix of topics.

✔ Choose a demonstration text at or slightly above the current benchmark level (F/G). We use *Hang On, Monkey!*, by Susan B. Neuman, but this text is interchangeable with others. Select a text that provides interesting information and engaging photographs. You may choose a big book or use a document camera to project pages during lessons (see Teaching).

✔ Prepare a new anchor chart titled, "How to Get Super Smart about Nonfiction Topics" (see Link). 👆

✔ Prepare today's strategy Post-it® note—"Take a sneak peek to start learning."—to add to the chart (see Link). 👆

✔ Display your "Readers Build Good Habits" chart from Unit 1 *Building Good Reading Habits*, as well as your most recent word-solving and partnership charts, such as "Reading Partners Work Together," from the previous unit (see Mid-Workshop Teaching and Transition to Partner Time.). 👆

✔ Refer to the "Good Habits for Solving Hard Words" chart from Unit 1 *Building Good Reading Habits*. 👆

✔ Ask students to bring one book that they read during workshop (see Share).

MINILESSON

CONNECTION

Invite students into the upcoming unit, creating fanfare around the chance to read nonfiction to learn about the world. Then unveil the nonfiction section of your classroom library.

"Readers, today is a special day. Today begins a new unit—on the *whole world*! You'll soar to outer space, swim with sharks, jam with rock bands, and play baseball with the pros! Who's excited to discover these new places and things with me?!"

Noting some doubt on the faces of a few children, I said, "You don't believe me? You aren't so sure it's possible? Let me show you the magic."

With fanfare, I lifted off the sheet covering the nonfiction section of the classroom library, unveiling labeled baskets of books. "In this unit, you are not only going to travel to new places and experience new things—you are going to do all that *and* become super smart about lots of different topics."

❖ **Name the teaching point.**

"Today I want to teach you that when reading nonfiction, or books about real life, readers start learning about a topic *even before* they read page 1. When they do a sneak peek, readers are *already* learning stuff about their topic."

TEACHING AND ACTIVE ENGAGEMENT

Recruit kids to join you in previewing the demonstration book that will thread through this bend, channeling them to glean information from just the cover. Reinforce the sneak peek strategy using guided practice.

"Let's try that together with this book, *Hang On, Monkey!* Let's take a sneak peek—we'll read the title and look at the cover—and right away, let's start learning about our topic, about monkeys. You ready?

"Let's get started. And when you learn some new information about monkeys, put your thumb on your knee! Read the title with me: *Hang On, Monkey!* Hmm, . . . Are you learning already?" I reread the title, looking thoughtfully at the cover: "*Hang On, Monkey!*" Scanning the room, I said, "I see a few thumbs—yeah! Absolutely.

"Let's look at the cover carefully." I pointed to the long tail on the monkey, coiled around the branch, and to the feet, perched on the branch.

"Are you learning some information? Good. I see many thumbs. Turn quickly to your partner and share all the things that you just learned about monkeys. Use your fingers to count the things that you learned. Go!"

Cite the work that one child did to provide an example, making sure the child took in many parts of the page. Explicitly name the importance of doing that.

"Oh, my goodness, you learned so much already, even before reading page 1! Abdul said he learned that monkeys need to hang onto trees. Thumbs up if you learned that, too. *And* he learned that they have tails *and* that baby monkeys can hang on to their mothers upside down. See that detail here in the photograph?

"Do you see that Abdul used information from the title *and* moved his eyes around the picture so he could learn about more than just one thing?"

Give children a second try, expecting them to benefit from your tip. After they look around the whole title page, share what another child did, extending that work in a way that models.

"Let's peek at another page or two and see what else you can learn before you even start reading the words!" Turning to the title page, I said, "Whoa! Let's read the title page," and I signaled for them to chime in as I touched the title and the author's name.

Hang On, Monkey! *by Susan B. Neuman*

"Remember to study all the parts of the page and to say *all* that you are learning about monkeys! Turn and talk."

To launch this unit, you will want to fill your room with enthusiasm, curiosity, and a sense of anticipation. Here, you set the tone and purpose for studying informational texts. It won't be a hard sell, but you will want to make sure that your students' energy is high for all the new books and learning that the class will do. This will greatly increase your students' levels of reading engagement.

Notice that instead of first demonstrating and then engaging the kids in a "try it," this lesson reverses that order—although actually there will be two try its! Keep them quick.

The children talked and I listened, and then I said, "Let me stop you for a second. You all are really thinking! Carla just said that she is learning that monkeys don't just walk on trees, they *hang* from them.

"Let's think together about what Carla said. 'Monkeys hang from trees.' Hmm, . . . What are *you* thinking about that?" After a second of silence, I said, "*I've* always thought they used their *tails* to hang, but this monkey is using its *arm*! Are you thinking more about Carla's observation, too? Fascinating."

Name what the students have done with one text that you hope they transfer to other texts.

"You already learned so much, even when you just did a sneak peek! You learned a lot because you didn't just look at the cover and the title page like this," and I made a fast, dismissive glance. "Instead, you looked like this," and I looked intently, slowly, up, down, and around the page.

LINK

Remind readers that they'll be learning about lots of topics as they read nonfiction books, and send them off to get started.

"If you, my nonfiction readers, do this every time you read, it will help you become super smart about lots of topics. You are going to learn lots of ways to get *super* smart about the world. I am going to start this chart":

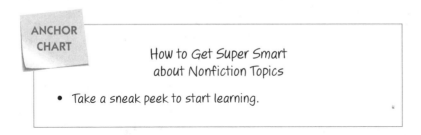

ANCHOR CHART

How to Get Super Smart
about Nonfiction Topics

- Take a sneak peek to start learning.

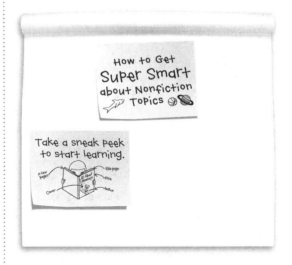

"This way we can keep track of all the ways we can study our books and topics!

"Before you go off to read, think about all the topics that are in your book baggie. You are going to become super smart about all of them. Remember, start learning even just during your sneak peeks, and keep learning as you read, read, read. Off you go!"

Moving from Reader to Reader Quickly, Spreading the Excitement of a New Unit

Rally children to do the new work while also assessing their current skills.

At the start of any unit, the conferring and small-group work tends to be quick, aimed to recruit the whole class into the most important work of the new unit. You'll want to move about the room as if you have roller skates on, angling kids to draw on all they have already learned to do, and also to give the new work of the unit a try. You'll want to allow for lots of approximation to build kids' energy for this new work and to help them expand their self-concepts to include the work of the unit.

As you do all this teaching, keep an eye out for those who seem to need something different. You'll need to do two things later this week. First, gather together the children who aren't being successfully swept along by the unit, and do whatever is necessary to make sure they are on a trajectory that is working for them. Also, think about whether your kids' assessment data suggest that you need to adapt plans for the upcoming unit.

Recruit kids to try the new work of the unit.

As you move among your readers, spreading enthusiasm for the new unit, you can also fan students' interest in the topics addressed in their books. For example, if you find a student who is oohing and ahing about bats, you might say to the children at her table, "Readers, do you know what Ella found out? She just learned that bats sleep *upside down* in trees! Isn't that awesome? Who knew?' I bet the rest of you are learning surprising things in your books, too. As you read, be on the lookout for information that can make the rest of us go 'Ohhhhh!'"

Of course, the main work of the reading workshop is reading. Continue to regard that as the number one essential of reading workshop and allow yourself to watch for the amount of engaged reading individuals actually accomplish. Face the facts. If some kids are dozing or chatting or spinning in circles rather than reading, you can't act like that is not the case.

Coach students on how to do a sneak peek.

You may decide to coach some students lightly by giving them some lean prompts and directions. You may say, "I'm going to watch you do your sneak peek. Talk about the

> **MID-WORKSHOP TEACHING**
> **Doing *Something* at the End of a Book**
>
> "Readers, eyes up here." I waited until the children were looking at me. "I want to remind you that when you are done with your book, you don't just throw it on the other side of your reading mat. Instead, you *do something* at the end of your book." I pointed to the "Readers Build Good Habits" chart from our first unit. "You might try to remember all the things that you already learned. You may even decide to reread the chart again so you can try to remember *more* things. Don't forget your strong habits!"
>
> **ANCHOR CHART**
>
> Readers Build Good Habits
>
> - Take a sneak peek at the beginning.
> - Check your sneak peek.
> - Do SOMETHING at the end.
> - Read MORE and MORE & keep track.
> - Set goals.
> - Reread to smooth out your voice.
> - Scoop up words in phrases.
> - Reread to see MORE.

"Readers, it's time to read with your partner. Let's do all the things that we did in our last unit in this unit, too. You still have your same partner as before.

"As you begin to stack up your books, start with a book that you haven't yet read, if you have one, so the two of you can discover it *together*! Partner 1, you will start off first today. Remember that when you are in a team, you decide together how you will read the book. You can echo read, choral read, or seesaw read!" I tapped the "Reading Partners Work Together" chart that listed optional ways to read with a partner. "Then it will be Partner 2's turn to go.

"I bet you'll find that two people can learn even more when you learn together!"

ANCHOR CHART

Reading Partners Work Together

- We work as a team. (sit side by side, book in the middle, take turns)
- We build good habits together. (sneak peeks, do things at the end of books, reread books)
- We read together. (choral read, echo read, seesaw read)
- We give reminders. ("Don't forget to . . ." and "Try this instead . . .")
- We grow ideas together. ("I never thought about that!")
- We give book introductions.
- We don't just tell—we HELP!
- We do SOMETHING at the end. (reread, smooth it out, retell, share ideas)

---

things that you think this book will teach you, and I will listen as you begin to study the cover and the inside pictures."

Then as the students begin, you may prompt in lean ways by saying, "Look at something else on the page," or "Think about what is happening," or "Name a few things you see." You might say, "Turn the page and keep thinking, 'What will this book teach me?'" Providing lean prompts when students need support is a way to provide some light scaffolding. Then say, "As you read now, you are going to find out what you were right about and what the book is actually teaching you. Then when you read the next book, don't forget to do the *same* thing. Do a sneak peek to get yourself ready to read!"

Remind kids to use the reading habits developed earlier.

Of course, while kids are embarking on the new work of the unit, make sure they continue to draw on the early reading habits they developed during Unit 1 *Building Good Reading Habits*. Many students will need quick, lean reminders, so plan on doing a few table conferences to remind them to draw on all they learned earlier. For example, if you observe a table of children who are slow to take out their books, you might say to them, "Readers, this is a unit on nonfiction reading, but does that mean you *forget* everything you already know about what readers do? No way! How many of you remembered to pile all your books up on your reading mat and then read right through that pile?"

As you listen to children reading nonfiction aloud, give them the same sorts of feedback that you gave earlier this year. You might, for example, say to one child, "You are really working hard to read your words. Remember not to mumble past words that you don't know; work at them instead!" That youngster may need to be reminded to keep his word-solving chart front and center. And, in general, it's a good idea to refer to charts that you and the class made during earlier units.

You will need to reach lots of kids quickly. So after you work with one child, you will probably want to broadcast that teaching more generally, turning a one-to-one conference into small-group work by saying to the entire table full of youngsters, "Readers, don't forget to work hard to look all the way through to the end of each word. Use our 'Good Habits for Solving Hard Words' chart from our last unit if you get stuck!"

Similarly, you will need to remind kids that the rereading they did earlier in the year is equally important now that they are reading nonfiction. If you notice one child rereading, you can celebrate that work in a way that nudges others to do the same. "I saw Raven decide to reread her book! Who else is thinking that they, too, can reread their books and learn even more?"

Sharing Topics of Study

Invite children to share with the class the topics they learned about today.

"Readers, choose a book that has taught you a lot about something, put the rest of your books into your baggie, and then come with your book to the meeting area."

Once kids had assembled, I said, "Let's start by sharing some of the amazing topics you learned about today! When I toss my magic fairy dust on top of your head, tell the class a topic you learned about that has fascinated you." I gestured to the books the children held. I started to wiggle my fingers together over Sabrina's head and then pretended to drop fairy dust right onto it.

After a second of absolute quiet, Sabrina said, "I love ponies." I responded, "You read about ponies today?" She nodded. "And you loved it?" She nodded again. "Did you become smarter about ponies?" She nodded. "Let's hear other topics." I headed to Thomas in the back row, and sprinkled the fairy dust.

"Trains." I said, "Wow, trains. Such an important mode of transport!"

When one child piped in that he, too, had read about trains, I said, "Similar interests. You two may need to talk about trains at lunch today!" I kept going, picking up speed, and children called out their topics: "Families." "The ocean." "Wolves." "School." Then I said, "I'll bet you learned lots of interesting things about your topics. Take a moment to think about what you learned from your reading today. Put your thumb on your knee when you have an idea." I waited a bit and then asked, "Sam, what did you learn about the ocean?"

"It's really, really big," Sam answered.

I said, "Interesting! What did you learn, Anita?"

"I learned that penguins eat fish," Anita said.

I responded, "Fascinating!"

Debrief. Ask children to share one fascinating detail about their topics with their partners.

"Do you see how many different things there are to study? Partners, take a minute or two to share some of the things you learned about your fascinating topic. Go!"

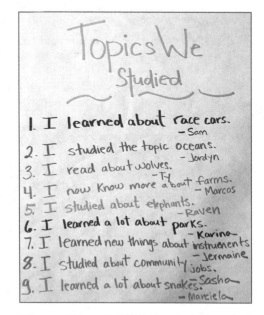

FIG. 1–1 This sort of list helps students reflect on what they read about, and suggests future reading ideas.

Studying One Page Can Teach So Much

IN THIS SESSION, you'll teach students how to linger on a page and use the pictures to find more details and information that accompany the text. You'll show students how they can slow down in their reading and name what they see before they turn the page.

GETTING READY

✔ Use a demonstration text, such as *Hang On, Monkey!*, by Susan B. Neuman, that you can project to the class, perhaps using a document camera (see Teaching and Active Engagement).

✔ Display the anchor chart "How to Get Super Smart about Nonfiction Topics" so it is ready to refer to and extend (see Link and Mid-Workshop Teaching). 👆

✔ Prepare today's strategy Post-it notes—"Stop and study each page." and "Guess what might come next."—to add to the chart (see Link and Mid-Workshop Teaching). 👆

✔ Keep the partnership chart, "Reading Partners Work Together," at hand (see Transition to Partner Time). 👆

✔ Create or display an information writing chart that shows strategies for how to add details and say more in writing. We use the anchor chart "How Can I Teach My Readers?" from *Nonfiction Chapter Books* in the first-grade Units of Study in Opinion, Information, and Narrative Writing (see Share). 👆

✔ Make sure students have a book that they have read in independent reading (see Share).

MINILESSON

CONNECTION

Celebrate that children are flying through books, but remind them that as writers, they've learned to slow down and add detail. Suggest they can do something similar as readers.

"Readers, yesterday you read and read and read. You were flying through books! Watching you read reminded me of watching you write. In writing workshop, you often write lots of books as well.

"But do you remember that lately I've been reminding you that because you are stronger writers now, you are ready to slow your writing down, to reread more often, and to add more details to your writing? Because here's the thing: the same is true for your reading! You *do* want to read a lot! *But* you also need to think and learn as you read your nonfiction books. When you read thoughtfully, that helps you get smarter about your topics."

❖ **Name the teaching point.**

"Today I want to teach you that readers who want to get smart about a topic don't just let the pages fly by. Instead, readers think, 'This *one page* can make me smart,' and they read each page closely, getting as much as they can out of it. They read whole books that way."

TEACHING

Recruit kids to join in shared reading of a page, then in scanning the picture. Note what you see in a few parts of the picture, framing what you notice as an observation about the topic.

"Let's look at page 4 in *Hang On, Monkey!* Let's read the words together, and then let's study the page, remembering that this one page—any one page—can make us smarter about the topic, about monkeys. Every time you learn something new, put your finger on your knee. You ready?" We read in unison:

This monkey hangs on a tree.

It lives in a rain forest.

northern muriquis

I read the text with the students. Although *northern muriquis* is a fancy, domain-specific vocabulary word, one that would be quite difficult for most first-graders to read on their own, I read that label to the illustration just as I read everything else. You may decide to say, after you read words such as these, something like, "Oh, that is the name of these specific kinds of monkeys. Interesting!"

"To learn a lot from this one page, to let one page make us smarter, we need to think about the words and to look closely at the page and say what we see."

I first reread the text, signaling when I learned that the monkey lives in a rain forest by putting a finger on my knee, reminding the children to do that when they learned something new. Then I looked at the picture, moving my finger onto parts of it and back to the print. I lingered a bit so that students could have an opportunity to think, and as I did this, I saw a few fingers on knees. "I see that Carla has already learned some more information," I said, replicating the gesture. Immediately, five other students put fingers on their knees.

"Here I go!" I slid my finger along the picture of the branch. "I see that the monkey has one arm and its tail both wrapped around the same branch. It's like the tail is another arm." I slid my finger back to the hand. "And look at the hand here. It's wrapped all the way around the branch. The hand and the tail do the same hanging-on job for monkeys."

I continued, saying, "Where should I look next?" I moved my hand over the picture, scanning the page with my finger and eyes. "Look at what I found—a baby! Let me zoom in closely to see what else I can learn about the baby. It looks like the baby is using its legs and arms to hold onto the mother, not the branch. Maybe babies learn to hold onto branches by first holding onto their mothers."

Debrief, noting what you did that you hope students are doing every time they read.

"Readers, did you notice that to learn a lot from even just one page, we didn't just let the pages fly by? Instead, we thought 'This *one page* can make us smarter,' and we read that page closely, with fingers and eyes moving across the page, thinking about what we saw, and getting as much out of it as we could."

ACTIVE ENGAGEMENT

Channel kids to read another page similarly, first reading the words in unison, then getting ready to share what they see and think with a partner.

"Let's try it again on a new page. Let's read together":

There are black horses.

There are gray horses.

FIG. 2–1   After reading *Colors of Horses*, Christopher reread each page and then looked at the picture to see what else he could learn about horses. Christopher commented as he read, "Here, the horse is in a race. And it is a fast horse with lots of muscles." On another page he commented, "These horses are work horses. They help out on farms moving things like hay." In both examples, Christopher found more information in the picture to help him think and say more about horses.

These monkeys sit on a tree.

They live in a grassy, open place.

vervet monkeys

"Time to stop and study this one page! Get ready to say all that you see to your partner!" After a minute I said, "Turn and talk." Once children started talking, I said, "Don't forget to say, 'This teaches me that . . .' What?"

LINK

Celebrate ways that children have engaged in an early version of close reading.

"I loved the way that you were moving your fingers to show what you saw on the page. Some of you counted five things you saw on the page! I even heard someone zoom in and talk about what monkeys looked like. You are getting good at studying one page. *And* you are getting smarter about monkeys.

"Readers, to become super smart about your own topics, you aren't going to just fly past the pages in your books anymore. You need to stop and study as you read so that you learn more." I flipped the page of the chart tablet over to reveal the reading chart that was started in Session 1 and added the new strategy Post-it.

"I'm sure you will find other ways to get super smart about nonfiction topics. And we'll add those to our chart, too."

Remind students how to set up for reading by stacking their books and getting ready to tally the number of books that they read.

As students went off to read, I voiced over to the class to settle into reading, just like they did in the last unit: "Readers, don't forget to stack up your books. Take a Post-it out and get ready to tally the number of books you read today. And remember to slow down and learn as much as you can from each page."

In reading, as in writing, one of the balances you are working to strike is that your students make their way through a high volume of texts while giving each one careful thought. This minilesson helps students recognize the importance of slowing down and noticing more on the page—and gives them a chance to practice doing this.

ANCHOR
CHART

How to Get Super
Smart about Nonfiction Topics

- Take a sneak peek to start learning.
- **Stop and study each page.**

Stop and study
each page.

Using Table Compliments to Create Energy around the New Work

TODAY, LIKE YESTERDAY, your conferring and small-group work will require you to put on virtual roller skates and move very quickly among your readers, rallying all of them to do the unit's work. One way to make a big impact on your class is to give what we refer to as "table compliments." To do this, first approach a table full of readers and draw a chair alongside the kids. You may find that when you approach, they stop working and look up at you as if to ask, "Yes?" You won't have anything to say when you arrive on the scene, so coach them to always continue reading and working when you pull in close, allowing you to study what they are doing. "Don't stop when I come near you as you are reading or writing," you can say, "because what I'm wanting to do is to study your work." This is one of many ways you can explicitly teach kids their roles in small groups and conferences.

Spotlight examples of students' successful application of reading strategies to reinforce them with other students.

If your intention is to give a table compliment, watch as kids work, thinking, "What is one child doing that I'd love to see the others doing as well?" It's especially great if the child who can be spotlighted in this way is *not* the class star, because setting that child up as a model can sometimes backfire. Say you notice that one reader is running his hand over the picture, either talking to himself as he does or in some other way clearly is reacting to the content of the page. You might interview that youngster to hear a bit about what he is thinking and then plunge into your table compliment.

Call for the group's attention just as you would for a mid-workshop teaching point. "Readers, eyes up here," you can say. As usual, wait until kids actually stop what they are doing and look at you. Then spotlight the child, making sure to name what that youngster is doing in a way that is transferable to others as well. "I want to admire the way that Leo is not just glancing at his page like this," you might say, "but instead, he is really studying the picture and adding the message in the picture to the message in the words. It's so cool because . . . Leo, what do the words say?"

(continues)

MID-WORKSHOP TEACHING
Predicting What the Upcoming Text Will Say

"Readers, readers, look this way." I waited. "How many of you have been reading in such a way that you get a *ton* of information from even just one page? Yes! Here's another thing you can get from one page. You ready? You can get *an idea for what might come next in the book*! Like if you read, 'There are many kinds of storm clouds,' then you might guess, 'I bet the next page will tell about some of those kinds of storm clouds.' And if you read a page that says, 'Some dogs are big, some dogs are small, some dogs are short . . .' the next page might say . . ." I paused dramatically, gesturing with my hands for students to chime in.

They chorused, "Some dogs are tall!"

"As you read one page, you can think, 'I bet the next page will tell about . . .' and then you can guess what might come next."

I added the new strategy Post-it to the chart:

ANCHOR CHART

How to Get Super Smart about Nonfiction Topics

- Take a sneak peek to start learning.
- Stop and study each page.
- **Guess what might come next.**

Guess what might come next.

TRANSITION TO PARTNER TIME
Helping Your Partner with Tricky Parts

I stood in the middle of the classroom beside our two classroom charts, "How to Get Super Smart about Nonfiction Topics" and "Reading Partners Work Together." "Readers, remember that as partners, you need to be *helpers*, and not just when your partner gets stuck on a word! You can also help your partner get *super* smart about his or her topic. What will you remind your partner to do?" I asked. I turned to the partnership chart and began reading it aloud with the pointer on the chart. The children joined the shared reading.

"Great, now look at your books and think, 'Are they all stacked up, ready to read?' Did you decide who will go first, Partner 1 or Partner 2? Did you pick *how* you will read your books? If you have, then you are ready to read and be super helpers! Don't let your partners just fly through their books!"

ANCHOR CHART

Reading Partners Work Together

- We work as a team. (sit side by side, book in the middle, take turns)
- We build good habits together. (sneak peeks, do things at the end of books, reread books)
- We read together. (choral read, echo read, seesaw read)
- We give reminders. ("Don't forget to" . . . and "Try this instead . . .")
- We grow ideas together. ("I never thought about that!")
- We give book introductions.
- We don't just tell—we HELP!
- We do SOMETHING at the end. (reread, smooth it out, retell, share ideas)

Leo might read, "The squirrel eats many things."

Then you might say, "And Leo, tell us how much more you learned by studying the picture and adding what you learned from the picture to what you learned from the words!" The important thing is to name what a child is doing in a way that pertains to other texts. In this instance, you won't just celebrate that Leo learned from the picture that squirrels eat fruit as well as nuts. Instead, you will note and celebrate that he gleaned information from both sources. Before you leave, invite others to try the same work that Leo is doing. As they get started, you might coach their efforts.

A table compliment like this requires just a few minutes of your time, but it can make a world of difference in helping students learn and apply new strategies. Early in most units of study, you can use this method of teaching to create energy around the new work of the unit.

Referring to Charts as Reminders

Compliment students on how they worked hard to slow down and learn more from each page.

"Readers, you've been working really hard on learning from your information books. You've been doing sneak peeks and studying right from the start! You've been stopping and studying the pages and trying to learn as *much* as you can.

"But you know what? It doesn't always work. It's not always easy to know what to say to your partner!"

Encourage students to consider how writing strategies might also help them as readers.

"So I thought we could talk about some *other* ways to help you and your partner think more about a book. In fact, we have some tools in this room that might help." I stood up and started to point to various charts. "I'm thinking this chart could help." I took the chart titled "How Can I Teach My Readers?" off the writing workshop bulletin board and placed it front and center on the easel.

> **ANCHOR CHART**
>
> ### How Can I Teach My Readers?
>
> - Think about questions my readers might have.
> - Include pictures (teaching words, lines and arrows, zooming in).
> - Give an example.
> - Use shape, size, and color words.

This chart, from Grade 1, Unit 2, Nonfiction Chapter Books *of the Units of Study in Opinion, Information, and Narrative Writing (Calkins et al.) can be a great tool for readers as well as for writers. During writing workshop, students learn to elaborate and say more in their writing. Students can also apply that skill in their nonfiction book talks, using similar cues to prompt reading more closely and thinking more deeply about the topics of their books. Channel them to study photographs and pictures in their books and to use the elaboration charts to say more about what they are learning about their topic. This cross-curricular work is important to support students in internalizing these skills and working on transfer.*

"Let me show you. I've put stars next to three of the writing strategies we have been using to help us teach our readers. These can also help us study and talk about our pages more. Look at the first bullet that I starred. 'Think about questions my readers might have.' Well, as a reader, we can stop on a page and ask questions and try to answer them." I opened up *Hang On, Monkey!* and asked, "How do the monkeys play? Maybe they chase each other up and down the tree." Then I looked back at the students and said, "Did you see how I said more here by trying to ask and answer a question using the page?

"Look at this one." I pointed to the starred strategy on the chart and then read, "'Include pictures (teaching words, lines and arrows, zooming in).' As readers, we should pay close attention to these in our books and talk about them. Let's read the third starred strategy. 'Use shape, size, and color words.' How would we use those, you might ask? Well you could read your page and study the things on it by describing what they look like in detail. *All* of these things will help you learn more and say more!

"Right now, try using *this* chart from our *writing* unit to see if it can help you *say* more about the pages you are reading! Partner 1, place your book between you and Partner 2. Read to Partner 2. Both of you, try to stop and study the pages together, saying what you see. If it gets hard to see more, give each other tips from 'How Can I Teach My Readers?'"

Session 3

Readers Learn More by Chatting about What's Happening

MINILESSON

CONNECTION

Invite children to review the anchor chart, "How to Get Super Smart about Nonfiction Books," noting the strategies they've been using.

Once the students had gathered in the meeting area, I began. "Readers, you've been working hard these past few days to get super smart about all kinds of topics." Gesturing to the first bullet on our anchor chart, I said, "Thumbs up if you've been studying the covers to take sneak peeks." The children signaled that yes, they'd done this, and I continued down the list of bullet points. "I'm pretty sure I have seen a lot of you stopping and studying each page and saying (in your mind) what you see. Am I right?" I looked for children to again use the thumbs-up signal to confirm they were doing this.

"So, readers, you've done a lot of good work to read the pages in your nonfiction books—and to learn a lot from those pages."

IN THIS SESSION, you'll teach students how to bring the information on the page to life. You'll show students how to use the images on the page or in their heads to imagine what is happening just before and right after the part they're reading. This inferential thinking will help students envision the information and learn more from the text.

GETTING READY

✔ Display the anchor chart "How to Get Super Smart about Nonfiction Books" so it is ready to refer to and extend (see Connection, Link, and Transition to Partner Time).

✔ Prepare today's strategy Post-it—"Chat about a page or the book."—to add to the chart (see Connection and Link).

✔ Use a demonstration text, such as *Hang On, Monkey!*, by Susan B. Neuman, that you can project to the class, perhaps using a document camera (see Teaching and Share).

✔ Keep the partnership chart, "Reading Partners Work Together," at hand (see Transition to Partner Time).

✔ Ask students to bring one book that they read during workshop (see Share).

Name the teaching point.

"Today I want to teach you that to get really smart about your topic, you don't just read a book—you also have little chats about that book. You read the words on the page, and then you use your *own* words and your *own* ideas to talk about the book (or the page) with yourself or with a friend."

I added the new strategy Post-it to the chart:

ANCHOR CHART

How to Get Super Smart about Nonfiction Topics

- Take a sneak peek to start learning.
- Stop and study each page.
- Guess what might come next.
- **Chat about a page or the book.**

"Chat about a page or the book."

TEACHING

Using a simple example, explain the idea that when one sees (or reads about) a person doing an action, the reader can often infer what has already occurred or will happen afterward.

"So, readers, if you're trying to get really smart about your topic, and the page says, 'Once the monarch butterfly's wings were spread wide, the butterfly flew to the nearest milkweed pod,' you don't just read the words on the page. You also *think* about what you can learn from the page, chatting about what's there (with either a friend or yourself). Sometimes, in those chats, you might think about what must have already happened or what might come later. So, if you read":

> Once the monarch butterfly's wings were spread wide . . .

"and you chat about that to yourself, what might you think? I might think, 'Maybe just before this, when the monarch comes out, its wings are all squished together.'"

Demonstrate this strategy, using the demonstration text that weaves through this bend in the unit.

"Let's do that sort of thoughtful reading with our book, *Hang On, Monkey!* Are you ready to read this page and have a little chat in our minds about what we learned?" I projected the page so that children could see it.

"Remember, we will read the page, and then we'll chat about what is on the page. And as part of that, we might think about what must have already happened or what might happen next. We'll use our *own* words and ideas to think and chat about the page."

It's important to help students do more than just restate what the information on a page says. You will want to teach students also how to infer and read between the lines. In this lesson, you'll teach students to go beyond naming what they see on a page to picturing in their minds what is happening. Plan to practice this type of work throughout the day, during read aloud, shared reading, and even during the content areas.

Although you are teaching readers to infer, it is not important for six-year-olds to know that technical vocabulary term. We don't use it with the kids. You can, of course, decide otherwise if you wish.

"Read this page with me." We all read out loud:

> This monkey hangs on a tree.

"I *see* the monkey hanging on the tree," I said. Then as if catching myself I said, "Oh, wait, that's what the *book's* words say. I need to use my *own* words to chat about what's happening. Maybe I'll think about what must have already happened or what might be coming next. Listen as I have a little chat in my mind. See if it matches what you were chatting about in your mind."

Assuming the role of reader, I said, "I see the baby monkey hanging on the big monkey's back. To get up there, the baby probably crawled onto the big monkey's back. Maybe the big monkey helped the baby up. I think the big monkey is going to keep swinging from tree to tree with its arms and legs and tail holding onto lots of branches. I bet that baby is going to hold on tight so it doesn't fall off."

I looked at the children and said, "See how I thought about the pictures *and* the words, and I thought about what must have happened before and what might happen next? I had a little chat in my mind about this page. Was that similar to what you were chatting about, or did your chat go differently?

"Quickly, turn and tell the person sitting next to you one thing you chatted about in your mind just now." I gave them just thirty seconds to do this.

ACTIVE ENGAGEMENT

Channel children to do the work you just modeled on the next page of the mentor text.

"Now it's your turn. Let's read this next page. As you read, get your brain going and try to have a little chat in your mind as you think about what's happening. Remember to use your *own words* in your little chat about monkeys. Read the next page with me." We read:

> Monkeys like to eat anything that smells good.

"Are you chatting with yourself, in your mind? Think about what must have already happened or what might be happening next? Use your *own* words." After I left time for children to think to themselves, I said, "Now try chatting with your partner."

I gave them a couple of minutes to do this, and then I shared bits of what I heard. "Wow, readers, you helped me to almost see this monkey—this snow monkey—moving through the rain forest and stopping to have a snack! Some of you were saying that you think after the snow monkey is done with this snack, it will look for other snacks. You are really trying to think about what is happening here and using your *own* words to say it."

Ask your students to read with you as often as possible. Enlarge print on a document camera or use a big book with enlarged print so that you can engage your students in a quick shared reading experience inside your minilesson. This gives students more time with their eyes on print in highly scaffolded material. This also creates another accessible text for your students—and especially your struggling readers. Make sure to maintain a captivating, fluent voice. Students will chime in and read along as best they can, when they can.

It is important that your students reread the class anchor charts with you often. Students will be more likely to use these if they know how to read them. This will be especially useful for more struggling readers.

LINK

Remind students to track their understanding by having a chat in their minds.

"You are becoming super smart information readers, doing everything you can to learn about all kinds of topics. Remember, it's important to study the words *and* the pictures. You can have a little chat in your mind (or with a partner) about the pages in your *own* words. You can try to say what you see happening. You might describe what might have happened before or what might happen next. These little chats will help you learn even *more* information!"

"As you go off to read, let's review all the things on our chart that remind us how to get smarter about our topics. Read it with me."

FIG. 3–1 Rereading the anchor chart

Helping Children Read Closely, Think Inferentially, and Maintain Learned Habits

Listen in and coach readers to do some close reading and inferential thinking as they read.

The minilesson from this session emphasized close reading and inferential thinking, and your leading of small groups and conferring with students should help to keep them engaged in this work. Jerome Bruner pointed out that any of the essential skills of a discipline can be taught to any child, at any age, and this minilesson aims to bring inferential thinking into the first-grade classroom. The goal is for kids to grow up knowing right from the start that good readers read between the lines. The text might say, "The monkey sits on a branch. Stomach full, he swings off into the trees, looking for the next meal." The reader is expected to fill in the gap, to infer that while sitting on the branch, the monkey had something to eat. If the reader knows from earlier in the book that this particular kind of monkey eats bananas, then it's expected that the reader uses that knowledge to imagine that the monkey is looking in banana trees for the next meal.

You can support this sort of inferential thinking in a number of ways. First, don't underestimate the importance of side-by-side reading. "Can I read along with you?" you can ask, pulling up a chair. You might say, "Let's read the words, and the picture, and say

(continues)

MID-WORKSHOP TEACHING
Rereading When You Forgot What the Text Says

"Readers, sometimes when you are reading, you go to have a little chat about what's on a page, but then you end up forgetting what *is* on the page! Your mind can get so full of your own ideas that you end up forgetting the whole book! If this ever happens to you, remember to go back to the last place where things were still making sense and reread."

TRANSITION TO PARTNER TIME
Thinking while Reading with Partners

"It's partner time! Partners, you have two readers. That's a lot of reading muscle," and I made a muscle, "so load up your reading mats. Before you start, however, two reminders: decide who is going to go first, Partner 1 or 2, and decide together *how* you will read." I gestured to the options listed on the chart "Reading Partners Work Together."

Once the kids had begun reading, I voiced over, saying, "I can see you thinking as you read! I see you read a page, and then before you turn the page, it's like all these thought bubbles come sailing out of your head. To make sure you're thinking, read our chart about things you can talk about while reading." I pointed to the anchor chart.

ANCHOR CHART

How to Get Super Smart about Nonfiction Topics

- Take a sneak peek to start learning.
- Stop and study each page.
- Guess what might come next.
- Chat about a page or the book.

"Make sure that, as you are reading and listening to one another, you work together to get smarter about your topics. If your partner is having a hard time saying something, offer a tip or a suggestion. You can even ask questions to help your partner get started. Be a helpful partner!"

what we're thinking." The youngster might go first, only reading the text that is literally on the page. You might nod and then demonstrate how you think beyond that. "And I'm wondering if . . . , aren't you?" you might say. "Do you think that maybe . . . ?" you might say. You could be more explicit. "Let's think about what he might do next. I wonder if there are any hints from earlier in the book."

Remind readers to continue using habits developed in the last unit of study, as well as those you addressed at the beginning of this unit.

Although part of your teaching will be aimed at supporting the new work of the unit, it's also important to help students regularly do all that they've been taught thus far—and all that their books require. For example, some of them will need you to remind them to reread to smooth out their reading, scooping up more words. Because your students will have moved into reading informational texts—and some will have progressed up a notch of text difficulty—you may find that some kids sometimes revert back to reading words one by one. You may say to those students, "Don't forget to reread that page and make your voice smooth. Let's try that right now."

Refer students back to the anchor chart from the last unit, *Building Good Reading Habits*, especially if they don't seem to have any ideas about what they can do when they finish a book. Hopefully, they will say, "I need to do something!" You can then ask, "What will you try?" You may even need to help the student make a short list of three options to choose from each time they finish a book.

Using Charts to Remind Readers of Ways to Think and Say More about a Book

Suggest that classroom charts can help children think and say more about their books.

"Reading partners, please gather in our meeting area and bring one book from your book baggies, a book you read today." The kids convened. "I once heard one partner say to the other, 'Squeeze your brain so you can make some ideas.' When I heard that, I thought, 'That's *just* what I try to do when I read! I study the page, and then I squeeze my mind, almost like it is an orange, only instead of making orange juice, I'm making thoughts.'"

Holding up an imaginary orange, I said, "Right now, squeeze a make-believe orange in your hand and get some pretend orange juice out of it." The children all did this. "Do you think that when you read, you can squeeze your mind to get some thoughts?"

The kids were game, so we read a page together and squeezed our minds to get some thoughts. We then proceeded to practice thinking and making inferences about *Hang On, Monkey!* and finished the book together.

Then I said, "Wow, we just squeezed a whole lot of information from the rest of this book. Now, in your own books, try the same thing. Do it with your partner. Go!"

Monkeys live and play together.

Readers Reread to Make Sure They Understand Their Books

IN THIS SESSION, you'll remind children that when readers finish a book, they should try to remember the whole book, not just individual parts. This session helps students reread to put the parts of their books together.

GETTING READY

✔ Use a demonstration text, such as *Hang On, Monkey!*, by Susan B. Neuman, that you can display to the class, perhaps using a document camera (see Teaching and Active Engagement).

✔ Ask students to bring a book that they have already read to the rug (see Link).

✔ Show an example of a book, either from your students' book baggie or from your leveled library, that uses labels in the illustrations or photographs (see Mid-Workshop Teaching).

✔ Ask students to bring one book that they read during reading workshop (see Share).

✔ Select one partnership to demonstrate to the class what good partners look like and do together (see Share).

MINILESSON

CONNECTION

Celebrate students' careful reading of their nonfiction books.

As students settled in around the meeting area, I started to clap, asking the kids to clap along with me, and then asked them to give themselves a big pat on the back, and then, finally, a cheer, "Hooray!" As the applause subsided, I began. "Readers, I wanted to start today's reading workshop with a little bit of celebration because I am so proud of your reading work—the way you're slowing down to study each and every page of your information books.

"You know," I leaned in to whisper, "some first-graders just fly through their books, swooping past each page like one of those bats that flies around in the night, not even seeing or learning much about their topics." The kids stared back, wide-eyed, as if in disbelief. "I know, I can hardly believe it! But *you* are being such careful readers to get super smart about the topics you're reading about." "Since you are so good at that, are you ready for something *new*?"

❖ **Name the teaching point.**

"Today I want to teach you that at the end of a book, readers think, 'What have I learned about this topic? Am I smarter about the topic now?' Then, they look back in their books and try to remember *all* that the book taught them."

TEACHING AND ACTIVE ENGAGEMENT

Invite students to look back at the text to remember what they have learned.

"So now that we have finished *Hang On, Monkey!*, let's ask, 'What have we learned about monkeys? How has this book made us smarter about that topic?' Let's think about the book and try to say four or five things to make sure we have learned as much as we can!" I started thinking to myself, tapping one finger, then another. With a fleeting gesture, I checked in that the class was doing similarly, and nudged the remaining children to join.

"I've thought of three finger-fulls already," I said. "Keep thinking." I signaled by holding up a hand.

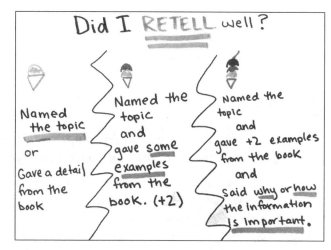

FIG. 4–1   This chart is a mini-rubric helping students think about retells at the end of reading their information books.

After another moment, I pulled the class back together. "I'm worrying that some things may have slipped my mind. Are any of you worrying about that as well? Because what readers often do is to look back or *reread* to remind themselves of things they've already learned.

"So let's first *look* back over the pages and look for information that we might not have remembered at first." I made a show of flipping through the pages and then said, "Oh, I am remembering more things. We can also reread. That will help us as well. Let's reread, so that at the end, we can really get as much information from this book as we can!"

I read the book aloud, placing it under the document camera so that children could see the pictures and join with me as I read the words.

Debrief, pointing out the transferable work that students have done by pausing at the end of a book to recall what they learned and rereading to glean even more information from the book.

Then I looked up and said, "Now that we have reread, you should remember even more. Partners, tell each other what you learned about monkeys from this book. Try to include details you missed the first time." I moved in to listen in to a few partnerships, offering small coaching tips, such as "Use your fingers," and "Try to say four or five things."

It is important to support the skill of retelling with first graders, who often read page-by-page, not synthesizing, and therefore only recalling the last part they read. Your running record data can help identify your students' needs as they retell. Tell your readers that one reason to reread is to remember and collect the things we have forgotten. As students reread, their retells should become stronger.

Then I convened the class. "After looking back at the pages *and* rereading, you remember even more things that you have learned. You see, it helps to stop at the ends of books and think, 'What have I learned?' It also helps to reread to fill in the missing parts. You are finding lots of ways to get smarter about your topics!"

LINK

Transfer today's teaching to students' independent reading by suggesting they get started reading and do what they've been taught when they reach the ends of their own books.

"The good news is that anytime you finish reading a nonfiction book (or even when you finish reading a big chunk of a nonfiction book), you can do this. Pause, think back, reread, and gather up all that you have learned. Then, later, you can help other people get smart about the topic! You can say to someone, 'Hey, did you know that monkeys . . .' or 'Hey, did you know that volcanoes, or ponies, or space ships . . .' You can teach others about your topics.

"Instead of heading back to your reading spots right away, let's start our independent reading time right here in the meeting area. Take out the book you brought with you. Start by thinking to yourself, 'What have I learned about this topic? Has this book made me smarter?' Use your fingers to try to remember four or five things you've learned. If you want, you can look back at the pages and reread, finding more things that you learned. Get started now."

I watched quietly as students started, noticing who was thinking quietly, remembering what they had read, and which students were rereading. I moved around the rug to briefly coach students on what I saw them trying.

After a few minutes, I voiced over to everyone, "I see lots of you working on rereading and trying to remember more! Remember to do this work on other days, whenever you finish reading a nonfiction book. That way you will be able to carry all you learn with you, and you can even say to someone else, 'Hey, did you know these things about race cars, or tigers, or trees? I just learned a *whole* bunch of stuff! Wanna hear?'

"Okay, keep reading, and when I tap you, go off to your reading spot and keep going!" I tapped students, one by one.

FIG. 4–2 Two students work on retelling during partner time.

Occasionally, it makes sense to ask students to start their independent reading at the meeting area so they can be close to you and you can more easily monitor and coach their use of the new strategy. Sometimes when kids immediately return to their usual spots for independent reading, they too easily revert to their usual habits, casting aside the minilesson in favor of their old routines. With kids gathered up close, you can easily observe and remind students to reread when it seems appropriate. Starting at the rug also has the added benefit of immersing students in the new work. Everywhere they turn, other kids close by are getting started. Don't overdo it, though! Many kids are easily distracted when sitting in a large group for too long.

Supporting Readers Who Fall below Benchmark Level

YOU'LL NO DOUBT want to provide the kids who are well below benchmark level with some extra help, and this is a good time to do that. Generally, as soon as a unit is well launched, this becomes the next priority.

Often when kids read well below benchmark level, the tendency is for a teacher to bring those kids into a small group and then support them to do work that is considerably beyond their zone of proximal development. This means that the kids who are well below benchmark level can become very dependent. They may find it very difficult to work independently.

Help children who read below benchmark level do work that is a notch above their own independent reading levels.

From the start, it is important to break that cycle. The first step is to figure out work that this group of kids can do that is just a notch above what they can do on their own. That way, you can plan to scaffold them for just a few days, lightening the scaffolds across those days, so that by the end of the stretch, you can send them off to

work independently at that level. If kids are well below benchmark, the level at which they can work independently won't be especially high, but it's important to mobilize them, to reverse their stagnation, and to show them that they can actually work at something, master it, and use it to good effect. Then you can return to ratchet them up another level soon.

You may have students who have been languishing at below-benchmark levels for a long time, and they will be your most urgent concerns. Pull these children into a small group. Perhaps you'll plan to work first with that group on highly supportive shared reading, doing that for two days in a row with a few texts that are just a bit beyond those readers' independent levels. That way, you can introduce them to a couple of texts that are just above their just-right book levels, so that through rereading and partnership time, those books can become "just-right reads."

Also, try to make sure that these children have opportunities for repeated practice with these strategies across the day. Look for opportunities outside of reading workshop

(continues)

MID-WORKSHOP TEACHING   **Learning from a Book's Labels**

Standing in the middle of the room, I said, "Readers, let me have your eyes up here. As you are reading, trying to remember what your book is about and what it is teaching you. I am noticing that some of you are paying close attention to *all* the words on the page. Many of your books have some super hard words that label things in your illustrations, explaining what they are."

Using the document camera, I displayed an example from one of the books that a student was reading. "Do you see here, in this book, how the things on this farm

are labeled? Read these labels with me." I gestured for kids to join and we read them together quickly. "This is so important to do, because it gives you even more information to learn!"

I returned back to the middle of the room, "As you keep reading, look out for the labels in your books. Don't skip them. Read them and learn even more."

Helping Your Partner See and Say More

Direct students to listen to and evaluate their partners, encouraging them to repeat, clarify, and/or elaborate.

I called students' attention so I could provide clear directions for today's partner time.

"Readers, to start off partner time today, Partner 2 will begin. Pick a book that you have already read, and put that at the top of your stack. This book will be the first one you retell.

"Partner 1, you will be listening to Partner 2. Make sure that you understand what Partner 2 is saying. If you don't, ask her to repeat it or to say it another way to make it clearer.

"Then, read the book together, with both of you trying to see and say more. Be on the lookout for more information that you can add. Partner 2 might have forgotten some pieces of information. Partner 1 may see more in the book to add. When you are done, see if the *two* of you can say more when you retell together. Try to use four or five fingers!

"After you are done, switch partners and do it *all* again! Ready, Partner 2? Go!"

After a few moments, I called out, "Partners, keep reading through your stack in this way. Don't forget to decide *how* the two of you will read together. Remember, before you read, retell the information quickly, and then help one another to see and say more!"

when you can work on things like tackling unknown words by checking the picture and using the first sound. Also, these youngsters can benefit from help using high-frequency words as anchors throughout the day. You might help them learn a few new "snap words" or high-frequency words during word study time. Then give students these new words on a word ring that they can read and use during reading workshop. You might even ask these students to bring their reading book bins to practice finding and rereading "snap" words during word study time.

Consider how writing workshop can reinforce reading skills.

Writing workshop can provide especially potent opportunities to advance the skills of these kids, or of any students. For example, students who are working on short vowel work in reading can work on this also when they are writing words. Say to students, "One thing that writers do to help them spell words well is to listen to the sounds and think about what other words they know that make those sounds as well. Let's make a book together and try that. Then you can try it in your own books that you are writing."

As you write a book together, give students that sample or a copy of it. They can place it in their book baggie and practice reading it during reading workshop.

FIG. 4–3   Word rings are made up of high-frequency words that students are learning and practicing. As students are introduced to new words, the words are added to the ring. Students can have individualized word rings to practice the words they most need.

Learning from Observation
Studying a Partnership's Moves

Focus students' attention on one partnership that has been having productive conversations.

"Partners, will you make a big circle in the meeting area and sit with your partner? Bring one of the books you read together today. Decide quickly and come over right away."

With the class settled in the meeting area, I began. "You have been working hard to get smarter about your topics. As I was watching you work with your partners, I saw lots of things that each of you did that *everyone* could learn from. Let's be researchers and study a partnership to see the smart things that other kids do with their partners—things you could do, too.

"Carla and Marco, will you go first? And readers, study the things *they* do, so that you can do them with your partners, too."

As the partnership began, I watched with the others and voiced over, "Cool. They are reading the words *and* looking at the pictures. Notice them really studying the pictures! Oh, and it looks like they are going to chat about what they are thinking. Let's listen and give a thumbs up if they do something terrific that you could do, too." As the duo started talking, I stage whispered, "I see they are taking turns."

A bit later I said, "Whoa, did you hear Carla ask Marco a question?" Then later, I added, "I wonder if Marco is going to reread that part. Oh, look at what Carla is doing. She is *reminding* him to go back!"

Then I drew the class's attention to what Carla and Marco did at the end of their book. "Uh oh, Marco is getting close to the end of the book. I wonder if he is going to pause at the end and remember all the things he has learned! Oh my goodness, look! He *is* doing that. Look at his fingers wiggling just a bit. I can see he is listing things he remembers across them." I held up my fingers and started to move them, too.

After thanking Carla and Marco, I said to the class, "Will you remember to do similar work in your partnership? What should you remember to do?" After I fielded several responses, I said, "Can you try those things one more time with the books you brought? Partner 1, take out your book. Let me see the *best* partnership work ever!"

FIG. 4–4   This partnership is demonstrating how partners can work together. The rest of the class is studying and naming what they do well.

Working on Fluency, Including Stress and Intonation

IN THIS SESSION, you'll teach children that when readers are trying to understand and recall information from their books, it helps to read with expression, making their voices smooth and lively.

GETTING READY

✔ Display the anchor chart "How to Get Super Smart about Nonfiction Books" so it is ready to refer to and extend (see Connection). ✊

✔ Prepare today's strategy Post-it—"Make your voice sound smooth & lively."— to add to the chart (see Connection). ✊

✔ Use a demonstration text, such as *Hang On, Monkey!*, by Susan B. Neuman, that you can share with the class (see Connection and Teaching).

✔ Ask students to bring their book baggies and reading mats with them to the meeting area (see Active Engagement and Link).

✔ Choose a book, from a student's baggie, that you can demonstate fluency with (see Mid-Workshop Teaching).

✔ Use a demonstration, such as *Hang On, Monkey!,* that you can read a page from with dramatic fluency (see Share).

✔ Ask students to bring a book to the meeting area, where they have some favorite pages or parts (see Share).

MINILESSON

CONNECTION

Congratulate children on their recent progress. Gently note that sometimes tone of voice can get in the way of retelling. Demonstrate what it sounds like to read with expression.

"Readers, many of you are getting stronger and better at remembering your information by rereading and by using your fingers to help you retell the information in your book. This is something that helps you get ready to share with your partner and others what you've learned about your topics.

"This is hard work to do. How many of you, though, sometimes still feel like it's hard to remember *all* of the things that your book is teaching you? I've been noticing something that might be getting in the way of your retelling and getting the *most* out of your books. I've noticed that sometimes your voices are sounding a little . . . boring." I picked up *Hang On, Monkey!* and read a section in a flat, monotone voice. "Reading like *that* can make it hard to remember details at the end. *But* if I read it in a way that makes the words sound lively and *important* . . ." I reread the same section expressively. ". . . It will be easier to remember that information."

❖ **Name the teaching point.**

"Today I want to teach you that to understand and remember the information in books better, nonfiction readers make their voices sound smoother and livelier as they read."

I added the strategy Post-it to the chart:

ANCHOR CHART

How to Get Super Smart
about Nonfiction Topics

- Take a sneak peek to start learning.
- Stop and study each page.
- Guess what might come next.
- Chat about a page or the book.
- **Make your voice sound smooth & lively.**

TEACHING

Invite children to read part of the demonstration text aloud with you, paying attention to their expression and aiming to sound like teachers or reporters.

"I'm going to reread part of *Hang On, Monkey!* You can read along with me. Let's imagine that we are all teachers or news reporters who share the news of the day on television. Let's read the words like they are so, so, so important. Let's give this reading some expression! Later we can check, 'Did our reading sound smoother and livelier?' Ready? Here we go!"

Together, we reread the first couple of pages of *Hang On, Monkey!* I placed extra emphasis on the words, *hangs* and *rain forest*, gesturing for children to do so, too.

Debrief. Point out that you emphasized certain words to make them sound important—and to sound like a news reporter.

"Did you see how when we read that part, we made the words *hangs* and *rain forest* seem really important by sort of punching them out with our voices? Do you think we sounded like a news reporter?

"We did, didn't we? And did our reading sound smoother and livelier? Thumbs up, if yes!"

Often when children read fiction, we say, "Make your voice sound like a storyteller," to help them understand what a fluent voice sounds like. Here, I get students to try using a "teacher's voice" or a "reporter's voice." Not only does this give kids an idea of what their reading is supposed to sound like, it also reminds them that their job as information readers and talkers is to report and teach.

ACTIVE ENGAGEMENT

Channel children to choose a book to practice reading with expression, placing stress on some words to make them sound important. Offer lean prompts as they work.

"Pick one book from your baggie right now to practice reading smoothly and in a more lively way. Start reading. If you hear yourself reading in a boring way, make sure you stop and reread, and try to emphasize some words so that they sound really important."

As students read aloud in the meeting area, I circled around, giving lean prompts and directions such as "Go back and make those words sound really important!" and "I'll read this page first, in a livelier way, and then you try!" I told students, "That sounds like really important information!" and "You made that sound smooth. Keep going, and do it on the next page, too." I asked questions too, such as "How did that sound? Okay, then go back and scoop up more words to make it smoother!"

"Readers, I hear many of you rereading and smoothing out your reading and making it sound more important and lively! Good job!"

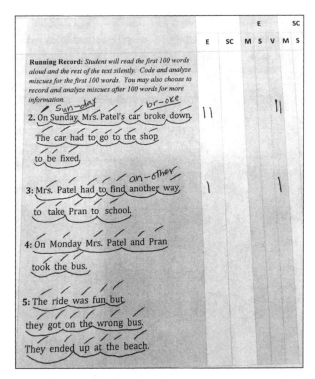

Even though this is a fiction running record, there are a few things you can help this reader notice and work on when reading either fiction or nonfiction, such as working on phrasing and stress, reading more smoothly, blending parts to say a word, and then checking that it all makes sense.

LINK

Reiterate the importance of the work children just did, reminding them that reading with expression will help them remember more information and show it off to the world.

"The work that you just did is important! When you read and reread until your voice sounds like a teacher or a news reporter, it helps you remember the information better. The more you do this, the easier it will be for you to retell even more of the book when you get to the end of it.

"But the thing is—you need to read aloud really well. Your voice needs to show the world that these are important words and the book has important information. It is almost like your *voice* can stand tall and proud. Right now, read aloud quietly in your head, and listen to yourself, making sure you aren't reading in a mutter. Make sure you are reading in a tall and proud voice."

Channel children to select a couple of books to share with a partner—to read and reread expressively and to retell, showing off what they know.

"Let's get ready for reading. Look at your stack of books right now, and pick a couple that you would like to share *first* with your partner today. These can be the first books that you read and reread today! Let's see if reading in this way will help you remember and retell more information. Then, when you get together with your partner, you can *really* show off what you know!

"After you finish the top books in your stack, go on to others. Off you go. Set up for your reading!"

FIG. 5–1 Mathew is reading through his stack of books during reading workshop. When he finishes a book, he places it in the next stack.

Supporting Children's Retelling and Recall Skills

Use retelling as an informal assessment, and pull students together in partnerships as needed to provide support for reading, thinking, and talking about books in ways that promote better understanding.

As you confer, listen to how your students retell and recall the information in their books. You may find that some students use the exact words in the book rather than their own or that they only retell the last page of the book.

Pull these children into a small group, asking them to bring their book bins with them. Set them up to spend group time working in their partnerships while sitting near other

MID-WORKSHOP TEACHING   Reading with Expression

"Eyes up here, readers. I have a tip for you. As you read, trying to make the words sound important, it helps to think, 'Is this information making me feel something?' Then you can make your voice show that feeling as you read." I held up a book from one student's book bin.

"Here, in this book, it says, 'Snakes slither to catch their prey.' Should I read that in a happy way, like this?" I read the sentence with an upbeat tone. "Or should I read it like this?" I reread it with a sense of anticipation. "Which way? Why?"

"The second way!" several kids called out.

"'Cause the snake's being sneaky!" one child added.

"I agree! The snake is being sneaky, so you can read it that way—sneaky!

"As you read your books, see if your book is making you feel a certain way. If so, read it that way! Doing this will also help you remember the information as you retell."

TRANSITION TO PARTNER TIME
Switching, Reading, and Talking through Books

"Readers, it's time to stack up books and read and talk with your partner. Today, let's begin with some echo reading to make sure that you're reading with your very best voices, like teachers and news reporters. Partner 1, you go first. Make sure that your books are stacked up, with the two books you will read first today at the top. Start echo reading to Partner 2, and *both* of you work on reading more smoothly and with a lively voice. When you finish the first book, see if the two of you can retell more information.

"When you're done, let Partner 2 read from his or her stack. Keep switching, reading, and talking through the books that you have stacked up on your reading mats. Go ahead and begin."

group members. Readers within each partnership can read together and then stop to discuss what they see happening in the pictures, talking especially about how that matches the words on the page. As partners read, you can work with one partnership for about a minute and a half, then the next, then the next, and then return to the first partnership. That way, you can shift among them, watching and coaching.

You may even play the role of a third partner, doing the same work you want the kids to do. By demonstrating how you think about what is in the picture and how that relates to the words, you can help students improve their work. Acting as a third partner provides a level of support that you can slowly withdraw. If you do this during your first interval with a partnership, when you circle back to that partnership, let the youngsters take the lead and just coach their work. You might say, for example, "Look closer," or "What does that make you think?"

At the end of the book, you can ask all the readers to retell the information once more. Then you can suggest that they progress to a second book, repeating the same thing. As students transfer their skills from one book to another, they internalize the strategy. They realize that you are not just setting them up to do good work with one book, but rather, you are showing them ways to read any book.

Often your small groups will last three days. You might do similar work on the second day, functioning as a third partner less and coaching more. If you pull the group a third day, you may decide to have students first work in partnerships, then on their own, thus moving them closer to being able to do the work independently.

Coach readers in a series of small-group sessions, using shared reading as a method of instruction.

You might decide to pull a small group of readers who need to work on moving from reading one word at a time to reading with better phrasing. You can use shared reading to provide extra work in fluency to this small group of students. Say to them, "I know that you are working on trying to read your books more smoothly. Scooping up more words with your eyes will help you sound smoother as you read. Let's all read this book together."

After the group work, you can give them each a copy of the book to reread throughout the week. Again, you will probably want to bring this small group together again, even if only to read a second book in the same way. Across the week, you can use shared reading as a way to get books into these readers' hands—books they can read with fluency. Each time you bring the group together, you might dedicate the last part of the session to giving students a chance to practice the smooth reading they have just done together, this time reading on their own in their just-right books.

Using Your Reading Voice to Convey Importance

Channel children to choose a favorite part of their books to share with a small group, showing off their best reporter's voices while their group assesses them. Model this yourself first.

"Bravo, readers! Are you sure you're a class of first-graders, not reporters and teachers? Your reading just now sounded so professional! In a minute, you'll have a chance to show off your reading voice. In a moment, you will get into small groups here in the meeting area and choose one of your favorite pages or important parts of your books. Then, you'll read with your best voice, giving a special punch to the words you think others need to pay attention to so they can hear what information is especially important. As you read, your group members can think, 'Does this sound like a reporter, smooth and lively? Or should you try again?'

"I'll go first. Will you indicate with your thumb up if you think I read smoothly and with a lively voice or with your thumb sideways if I should try again?" I read aloud the next part in *Hang On, Monkey!* with an animated voice, emphasizing certain words. Students gave me a thumbs up. "See how I gave an extra punch to the words *grassy, open place*?

"Now, it's your turn. Row one partners, turn to row two partners behind you. Row three partners, turn to row four partners behind you. Pick who goes first. Read the book you brought in the smoothest and liveliest voice you can. Everyone else in your group will listen and give you a thumbs up or sideways. Then let the next person in your group go. Let's do this quickly, so everyone will have a chance. Go!"

FIG. 5–2 Students are assessing the fluency work the class just did in shared reading. Thumbs up means that they have done a good job at sounding like reporters. Thumbs sideways means they need to try again.

A Celebration of Learning

MINILESSON

CONNECTION

Let readers know that you think their growing expertise on so many topics is worthy of a celebration.

"Readers, you have been reading and rereading your nonfiction books, getting smarter and smarter about a whole lot of different topics. We have *so* many experts in the room, about *so* many different things. Yesterday, as you were rereading your stack of nonfiction books with your partner, I was watching you closely and listening to just how much you know. I was fascinated by the things you were discussing.

"I began to think, we need to have a party! We need to celebrate and share *all* the smart things that you now know!"

❖ **Name the teaching point.**

"Today I want to teach you that when grown-ups are at parties (like a pizza party or a tea party), they don't just eat. They also talk—and often they talk about books they've been reading and new things they've been learning. You can have fun talking about books, just like grown-ups do, by sharing important information and interesting ideas and asking questions about your books."

IN THIS SESSION, you'll congratulate students on all they have learned. Your students will celebrate their new knowledge by talking with their classmates about what they have learned from their books.

GETTING READY

✔ Make sure students bring a book they have been reading to the rug for the celebration (see Active Engagement and Link).

✔ Display the anchor chart "How to Get Super Smart about Nonfiction Books" (see Conferring and Small-Group Work, Mid-Workshop Teaching, and Share).

✔ Display the chart "How Can I Teach My Readers?" from *Nonfiction Chapter Books* in the first grade Units of Study in Opinion, Information, and Narrative Writing (see Conferring and Small-Group Work).

✔ Give students an oppotuntity to swap books that they are chatting about (see Mid-Workshop Teaching).

✔ Gather Post-it notes to give to children to record their goals (see Share).

TEACHING

Demonstrate the way that grown-ups talk about topics they're learning about when meeting with other grown-ups.

"The other day I had a pizza party with some of my friends, and we got to talking about some of the reading we'd been doing. We started talking about the pizza, but that got us started talking about other topics. The conversation went a little like this":

Me: I'm just going to order my usual—a cheese pizza. I'm like monkeys. Do you know what I read the other day? This book said that monkeys eat the same thing almost every day.

My friend: Really? What else did you learn?

Me: Well, what really surprised me was that monkeys also play, just like little kids. Isn't that interesting?

My friend: Amazing. I wonder if we would see them playing if we visited the zoo.

Me: I'm sure we would. You're never gonna guess what I know about how monkeys move. It's really the most amazing thing. Do you want to know?

"See how we just got to talking about our books, saying things like, 'What surprised me the most was . . .' and 'What else did you learn?' and 'You're never gonna guess what I learned about . . .' Sometimes people talk like this at parties, making what they learned from books sound like the most interesting and fascinating things in the world!"

ACTIVE ENGAGEMENT

Invite partners to have a pretend tea party or pizza party, in their spots on the rug, chatting with each other about the topics of their nonfiction books.

"So, for the start of workshop today, you are going to have a party where you also get to *walk* and *talk* about *all* your topics, like experts." I stood up, began walking toward one of the corners in the meeting area, and pretended to sip tea. "People at these parties usually talk in an important way, like 'Oh, Marco, do you know what I read the other day? Really! I wouldn't be surprised if . . . Once I saw . . .'

"Before you get up and *walk* and *talk*, like you are at a tea party, or maybe a pizza party, will you just try it with your partner? Pretend you are at a tea party or a pizza party and try to talk about your topic in an interesting way!"

I gave children a chance to talk to their partners about their topics.

Sometimes, at the beginning of a unit, it is good to build momentum by having a short celebration of the work readers have accomplished thus far. You may want to liken this celebration to a pizza party or a tea party, where guests get an opportunity to chat about what they've learned. Have fun with this role play, and highlight just how much students have learned about the world so far in this first part of the unit.

FIG. 6–1 Students chatting about *Tuti's Play*: "In this book, this girl is in her school and she is in a play. And in her play there is a lot of dancing. Did you know that they get to wear lots and lots of make-up and dress up in the prettiest dresses that are gold and stuff?"

Name some of the ways you overheard children talking about their topics, helping them grasp the language of how people chat about new knowledge and react to it. Then encourage kids to keep talking.

Intervening, I said, "Listen to what I heard some of you saying at this party." I gestured to a small group of students and repeated bits of their conversations. "Sarah said, 'Do you know what I read? Elephants have the best memories.' And then Jake replied, 'Really?! I've never seen an elephant, but I bet if it saw me, it would never forget me!' Keep chatting."

I gave the kids some more time to talk and then stopped them to share another student's comment.

"Listen to what I overheard at this tea party over here. I heard Sam say, 'I just read all about riding waves. Once I rode a wave for a super long time. You have to balance well. But kids shouldn't go on really, really big waves. It's just too dangerous.' Sound interesting and important? It is!"

LINK

Invite children to walk and talk like they are at a party, circulating and discussing their topics with other kids in the room.

"I think you are ready to have a party! You can pretend you are sipping tea, or you can pretend you are eating pizza. I have set up a few different areas to sit or stand and talk about your topics." I pointed out the party spots.

"When I say, 'Walk and talk,' find a new area and new people to chat with about your topics. Of course, you can use your books to help you remember what you want to say or to help you say more."

Here are some things to do if you smell smoke or see fire:

1. Feel a door before you open it. If it feels hot, do not open it.

2. Stay low to the floor. Smoke rises.

 3. Call 9-1-1, but only for real emergencies!

4. If you think there is a fire in your house, stay outside the house.

5. If your clothes catch fire: stop, drop, and roll.

FIG. 6–2 Students chatting about *A Day at the Firehouse*: "Hey, do you know how to stay safe in a fire? Yeah, you should first feel a door, before you open it. Know why? In case there is more on the other side. Did you know you should crawl on the floor? You know why? Because then it's less smokey."

Lifting the Level of Student Talk and Assessing Their Learning

As students talk in small groups, confer with them to facilitate dialogue and lift the level of their conversations.

As you observe a student talking about her topic, you might suggest to listeners that they be skeptical when they hear a fact or a piece of information. Say, "Sometimes, people at a party don't believe all that they hear. They might say, 'Hey, how do you know that?' or 'Really? Prove it! Where did you read that?' Want to give this a try? Sarah, share your information again, and then let's all listen and respond with one of these questions. Let's see if Sarah can show us how she knows her information. Are you ready?"

Just as you do during your read-aloud book talks, make it a point to circulate to a few conversations and whisper in, responding or raising questions. You might whisper in the ear of a child, "Do you understand what that means? Ask her, 'What do you mean?'" Or you might whisper, "I've never heard that before. You? Ask him about that. Why does . . . or How does . . ."

You also may whisper in to help children begin their conversations. Notice what topics your students are discussing, and then prompt, "Have you heard that when you're racing cars . . ." or "When I was reading about families . . ."

Use the anchor chart to assess readers' knowledge of the strategies you have taught across this bend, and coach them accordingly.

On this last day of the bend, take stock of what your students are now able to do, and note any skills that might need additional support in the next bend. The anchor chart will be a helpful tool as you research individual students as well as partnerships. Look at your anchor chart and ask a few questions to check whether students are practicing the strategies you've been teaching.

MID-WORKSHOP TEACHING   **Bringing All You Know about Learning as You Read to a New Book**

"Readers, you all have shared and talked and chatted *a lot* about your topics that you are experts on! I bet you heard about some other topics that now interest you! I bet there are some books that *you* are now dying to read! Thumbs up if I'm right!

"I thought so! I'm going to give you just a couple of minutes to swap books with one another. If you want to go to the library and find books on a particular topic, that's fine, too. Then head to your reading spot to read on your own.

"As you start to read your *new* books on your *new* topic, don't forget all the things you just learned about how to study those books to get smarter!" I pointed to the anchor chart. "Let's read this list together."

Chatting Like Experts about a Topic

Ask partners to choose a book to read together that they can later discuss as experts.

"Readers, get together with your partner. Stack up your books, with the ones you want to read first on top. Partner 2 will go first today. Don't forget to decide *how* you will read your book! Then, after you read, you can *both* chat like experts about your topic, just like you are a grown-up at a party."

Then coach children based on what you observe, either in individual conferences, table conferences, or partnership conferences. Aim to help students do whatever they are not yet doing as they read. Typically, you may see many kids still just naming things on the page and not really picturing what happens. Others may be looking at the picture but be unsure what to say about what they see.

You might say to a table of children, "I like how I see Ella stopping and studying the page. Are you all remembering to do that? Great! Remember to do that *a lot* as you read. But *also*, remember to say what you see happening *or* use the 'How Can I Teach My Readers?' chart from writing workshop to help you describe the things in the picture with more words." Pointing to the chart, you might then say, "Try that right now on the page you are reading. Pick one of these things and just say it out loud to yourself. I'm going to come around and listen to each of you reading and thinking about your page. Don't forget to use the chart to help you think about what you can *say* about what you see!"

Ask students to reflect on their own progress using the anchor chart to guide them.

You may decide to have some children use the anchor chart to self-reflect. Ask, "Can I hear what you are thinking about this page? What can you do to see more on the page and say more about it? Let's look at our chart together and decide. What kind of thinking work can you do? Let's try that now!" Stay with the reader and coach him through the next few pages.

You can do the same type of conference with a partnership. You may ask the partnership, "Do you think you two can study your books more? How would you do that? Let's use our anchor chart and make some choices. What can you do to say more? Are you ready? Let's try!"

Celebrating New Strategies and Setting Goals

Invite students to reflect on their learning during this bend and to set goals for future nonfiction reading.

"Readers, you've worked so hard this week, and you've learned so much as well. Isn't it incredible how many things there are to learn about in our world? You have a new book or two already. And next week you can shop for a whole *new* bunch of books on *new* topics, so be thinking about what you want to study next. What else piques your interest? What else are you curious about in the world?

"Since it's a celebration day, I thought we could spend the last part of workshop celebrating your accomplishments as readers and setting new goals for the days ahead!

"Look at our chart, 'How to Get Super Smart about Nonfiction Topics.' These are reminders of things to do to study books." I put up three note cards on the easel and said, "With your partner, talk about which things you do *every time* you read, which things you do *sometimes*, and which things you may *forget* to do when you read. Then, decide on a couple of goals you want to try to do *every time* you read. Turn and set goals with your partner."

Reconvene the class. Share a few examples of goals that children made. Then ask the class to record their goals on Post-it notes.

"Readers, listen to Carolina's goal. She said, 'I forget to do sneak peeks because I get so excited to read. I am going to try and make that an *every time* goal.' And Sam said that he sometimes remembers to retell the whole book but not *every time*. It sounds like he found an *every time* goal, too. If you haven't already done so, tell your partner what your goal or goals will be. Then jot your goals down on Post-it notes and put them in your book baggies. That way, each time you are reading, your goals will be there as a reminder."

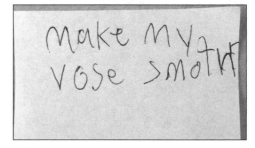

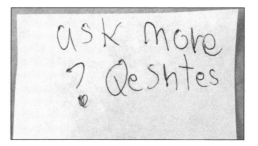

FIG. 6–3 Students can jot goals quickly on Post-its or index cards. This need not take much time or space.

Tackling Super Hard Words in Order to Keep Learning

Readers Don't Let Hard Words Get in Their Way

IN THIS SESSION, you'll remind students that readers are persistent, especially when they get stuck on hard words in their books.

GETTING READY

✔ Make sure students have new books in their baggies for independent reading (see Connection).

✔ Choose a text that you can display to the class, perhaps using a document camera. We suggest using a level G or H book. In this session, we use *I Want to Be a Doctor*, by Dan Leibman (see Connection and Teaching and Active Engagement).

✔ Cover a few tricky words in the text with Post-it notes (see Teaching and Active Engagement).

✔ Display the word-solving chart "Good Habits for Solving Hard Words" from Unit 1, *Building Good Reading Habits*. Remove any strategies that are no longer pertinent to the students or the current unit (see Teaching and Active Engagement, Mid-Workshop Teaching, and Share).

✔ Write or show a sentence from one of your student's books. Cover up one of the words in that sentence so that students can work together to generate other possibilities (see Share).

MINILESSON

CONNECTION

Demonstrate giving up on a text because of difficult words, and rally students to persevere in trying multiple strategies when words are hard.

"Readers, we start a new bend in our unit today. *And* you get a whole new baggie full of books, full of topics that you can learn about. I know you are going to learn a whole lot from your books. How many of you think you will learn a lot from each page *and* from your whole books?" The children signaled.

"The books in your baggies are full of cool things, and you will be able to become experts on a whole lot of new topics. But there's one problem. As you get stronger and stronger as readers, and as your books get more full of fabulous information, they also get more full of . . . challenging words. Today, you might just pick up a great book, planning to learn a lot from it, and find your reading goes like this." I opened a book, exclaiming "Oh, great! A book about doctors!" And I read.

> *Doctors help you stay . . .*

I stopped in my tracks, seeming paralyzed by the word *healthy*. I looked at the class, then back at the word, then back at the class, with an overly worried look on my face. Then I threw my hands up and said, "I don't know that word," and slumped in my chair, giving up. I tossed the book to the side saying, "This book doesn't teach me *anything* about being a doctor!"

Then I looked up and said, "It's like you are doing an obstacle course, and you get to a mountain of tires to climb, and you just stop and say, 'That's too hard.'

"Has that ever happened to you? You start reading along just fine and then—whoa! There's a super hard word right in your path. Have you ever come to one of those super hard words and thought, 'This word is just too hard. Forget it!'? Thumbs up if so!" Around the room, thumbs went up.

"How many things did you see me try?" The children looked at me with blank stares. Some looked at one another, and some just shrugged their shoulders.

❖ **Name the teaching point.**

"Today I want to teach you that nonfiction readers don't let *anything* get in their way of learning a lot about their topic—not even super hard words. They use everything they know to figure out those words."

TEACHING AND ACTIVE ENGAGEMENT

Invite students to help figure out tricky words you've covered by thinking about what would make sense in context and then looking at all the parts of the words.

"Let's all read this book about doctors and use *everything* we know to figure out the hard words. I've chosen a few words to cover, so we will all have to work hard to figure them out. But are we going to let those words keep us from learning a lot? No way! Let's rise to the challenge here and use everything we know to figure out those words. Ready to work? Ready for our new challenge?" I read:

> Doctors help you stay _____.

"Shout out different things this word could be." I fielded several responses, using my hand to call for readers to brainstorm more and more possible ideas.

Children called out a bunch of words: "Alive!" "In school!" "Good!" "Healthy!" "Not sick!"

"Okay, we've thought of many words that seem to fit and that would make sense. Do we just say, 'That's all we can do!'? Do we guess, and that's all? No! We also look at the first part of the word. Readers do that. Let's read the first part of the word, and then reread the whole sentence to think what the hard word could be."

> Doctors help you stay heal__.

You'll want to be sure students have plenty of books in their baggies and have changed these books at least once. Students can change books about once a week or when you think they are ready for a new set.

Exaggeration can be a great teaching tool, so by first showing a look of worry and dramatically slumping in the chair at the word healthy, *I underscore that giving up is not what any student would want to do in a similar situation.*

In Teaching and Active Engagement, you want students to generate a few words. The point is not to be perfect and guess the word exactly, but rather to develop flexibility and use meaning to help generate possibilities.

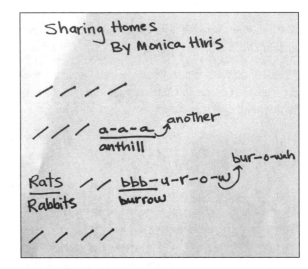

There are a few things to notice about the errors in this informal running record. The reader tries only one thing—to word solve. The reader does not cross-check or try to use the parts of words in many errors (2/3). You could use this lesson to teach the reader how to look at parts and reread to make sure that what he says makes sense. Also, you could ask the reader, "Do you know what a burrow is?" and if the answer is no, show it in the picture and tell the reader how to say the word. If the reader says, "Yes, it's the home for a rabbit," ask him to go back, reread, and make sure that what he read and said looks right and makes sense.

I ran my finger under the first few letters in the word, and with a few kids joining in, read the start of the word incorrectly, pronouncing it "heel" with a long /e/ sound. Then I read the rest of the sentence, without yielding a word that made sense. I threw my hands up to show this was too hard and said, "I give up. That's a super hard word."

Then, self-correcting, I pointed to "Try it 2 ways" on the "Good Habits for Solving Hard Words" chart and said, "No, wait. I'm not going to just give up. I'm going to try again. This time I'll say it a different way." This time I read the sentence, and said "heal" as /hel/, and then said, "Could the hard word be *healthy*? That's related to healing, but it fits better. Let's look at the ending." I peeled off the remainder of the Post-it note to affirm that try. "Let's reread to check if that word makes sense."

> Doctors help you stay healthy.

"*Healthy* looks right, sounds right, and makes sense! Let's keep reading."

We continued to read the text together, like it was a shared reading book. We stopped on a couple more covered words and repeated this process to solve them.

Debrief. Point out that the class tried several things when challenges arose. Invite children to review the anchor chart.

"Readers, do you see how when we were reading, we didn't let a hard word stop us from reading on and learning? We tried a few things to figure out the word, and we rose to the challenge! You can't forget all we have learned about solving words. Let's read over our 'Good Habits for Solving Hard Words' chart."

ANCHOR CHART

Good Habits for Solving Hard Words

- Check the picture.
- Look at ALL the parts of the word.
- Get a running start.
- Check it! Do a double-check!
- Try it 2 ways!

LINK

Send kids off to get started reading a new stack of books, with the reminder to persevere when they encounter unfamiliar words.

"Readers, you have a whole new set of books in your baggies, so you are bound to run into *longer* and *harder* words. When you read today, if you are reading along just fine, and then—Whoa! There's a super hard word right in your path—are you gonna think, 'This word is just too hard. Forget it!'?

"No way! Remember that nonfiction readers don't let anything get in their way of learning a lot—not even super hard words. Don't give up! Rise to the challenge. Imagine it's like climbing up that big mountain of tires! It's hard at first but feels great once you've done it! Use everything you know to figure those words out the best you can!"

Coaching Readers to Use All That They Know

Remind kids to use all that you've taught, in this unit and in past units, to understand their books.

Today begins a bend in which your minilessons focus on helping kids be more active problem solvers when they encounter tricky words. It will be important that a portion of your conferring and small-group work reminds readers to continue drawing on all that you have already taught. Be especially aware that children will be encountering a whole stack of new books, reading them for the first time. Therefore, it will be especially important that they take a sneak peek into those books, orienting themselves to the books' topics and to the way the books seem to be organized.

In your conferring and small-group work, try to remind kids to keep using the same strategies they learned earlier in the unit, such as taking a sneak peek even before they read page 1 and reading each page closely, getting as much as they can out of it.

Use assessment data to inform your plans for small-group work, including guided reading, to help readers move up book levels.

Meanwhile, devote some of your instructional time during reading today to helping students become more active word solvers. In preparation, study and analyze your running records and think about who is ready to move up the trajectory of text complexity. Select a small group and get ready to coach your readers.

You may decide to start a guided reading group of students moving into a new level. For example, you will probably have a group of readers nearly ready to read level G. Bring these students together and give them a book introduction to a level G nonfiction book. Most importantly, in your book introduction, support students by telling them the gist of what the book is about, what information they will learn, and what they should try to discover by the end, being sure to leave some work for students to figure out on their own. As students read, give lean directions and prompts, supporting them in using different sources of information to solve words. At level G, in particular, it is important that students begin to fix their miscues at the point of error.

MID-WORKSHOP TEACHING **Don't Get Stuck in the Mud! Backing Up and Taking a Running Start**

"Readers, eyes on me." I waited. "Watching you just now, I noticed that as you read along, you are getting stuck sometimes. You are not moving. It's like your feet are stuck in the mud.

"Remember, when you get stuck on a hard word, you can back up in the sentence, go to the beginning, and get a running start. Reread the sentence and think to yourself, 'What might this word be?'

"Then look at the first part of the word and say that part aloud like we did with *healthy*. Do it again and again—saying the first part of the word one way, then another way, and trying to think, 'What could it be?'

"And you know what? If you *really* can't figure it out, you can mark that part, and later when you read with your partner, the two of you can try to figure it out together." I pointed to the "Good Habits for Solving Hard Words" chart. "Remember, you can always remind yourself to use the strategies on this chart when you are stuck."

ANCHOR CHART

Good Habits for Solving Hard Words

- Check the picture.
- Look at ALL the parts of the word.
- Get a running start.
- Check it! Do a double-check!
- Try it 2 ways!

TRANSITION TO PARTNER TIME
Helping Each Other Do Word-Solving Work

"Time for partner reading. Right now, all Partner 1s, show me your muscles!" They did. "Now Partner 2s, show me your muscles!" They did. "That is a lot of muscle power. With all your combined muscle power, you should be really good at rising to the challenge of figuring out the hard words.

"So, Partner 1, look at your stack and start with book one, reading on your own. Partner 2, don't just jump in to help. Give Partner 1 a chance to do something—*anything*—to figure out hard words. But if Partner 1 *still* needs help, use your combined muscle power to work on the challenge together. Then switch, and Partner 2, you read the first book in your stack.

"See if you two can read through several books in your stacks in this way."

When students make an error, see if they realize it and try to fix it. If not, prompt them with questions to help them understand why it's an error. For example, you might prompt readers by asking, "Did that make sense?" especially if they mumbled through the word. Or if they said a different word in place of the one in the text, you might prompt readers by asking, "Does that look right to you? Is that what it says?" Students can then reread the text, thinking about what would make sense, or reread the word, breaking it into parts, to figure out what the word is.

After you support students in reading through the text, invite them to talk briefly about what they learned and what they think the book was mostly about. Then give students an explicit teaching point, perhaps going back to revisit a couple of words that they got particularly stuck on and had a hard time solving.

Depending on the needs of the students, your guided reading session might end with a bit of word work. You might take out a white board and place a few words on it. Have students talk about what they notice about the words and what is the same and what is different about them. Teach them something about the phonics features that can help them distinguish the words. You may even ask them to spell other words that are similar to those on the board. Then have the students reread the text and prompt them to find and read the word in context.

Most guided reading sessions will end with an explicit, transferable strategy. For example, you might say to your students, "As you're reading, make sure you check the words that you read. Check not just the first letter, but the *whole* word. Then make sure it *also* makes sense." Remember to keep track of the time you spend with each guided reading group; aim for ten minutes. In general, it's better to reach more students than to spend fifteen or twenty minutes with one cluster of three or four kids.

Working Together to Solve Hard Words, Drawing on Lots of Strategies

Invite the class to help you read one partnership's book, using the strategies they know to solve tricky words.

"Readers, who has strong muscles for figuring out the hard words? Show me!" They did. "Wowie! Let's use that combined muscle power to read some of your books together during our share, okay? This book belongs to Leo and Jonas, but they said we can all take a turn with it, okay?" I showed the class the book.

"Leo told me that this book has some tricky words in it. But I think we can use some of our strategies to tackle them together!" I pointed to the anchor chart. I began reading the book and then stopped at a word on the second page. "Yikes, this is a challenge. It says that trucks have powerful _____ to help them pull heavy loads. I think I'm stuck! Do I just give up?"

"No way!" the kids shouted. I nodded. "We are up for the challenge! Help me out. Turn and tell your partner what strategy we could use to tackle this tricky word!"

The students talked to their partners, and I listened in. I stopped them after about thirty seconds. "I heard Carla say that we could think about what makes sense in the sentence. Let's try it! The truck is using something to pull heavy things. What do trucks use to make them go? They have tires, wheels, I don't know, there are a lot of words it could be. I'm still not sure. We may need to try something else."

"Look at the first sounds!" Marco suggested. "Let's try it. Everyone make the first sound, I responded." The classroom erupted in chants of "mmmm" and "mo!" "Now we know its something that starts with *mo* that makes trucks go. What could it be?"

"Motors!" several students said. "Does that make sense in the sentence? Let's try it, I said."

   Trucks have powerful motors to help them pull heavy loads.

"Yes!" They all nodded.

"Wow! Its a good thing we didn't just give up! We tried a couple different strategies, and we were able to figure out that word! Great job using your word muscles!"

Session 8

Crashing Word Parts Together to Solve The Whole Word

MINILESSON

CONNECTION

Remind students to keep trying strategies when they get to a tricky word.

"When you are reading your books, sometimes you come to a super hard word, right? In fact, sometimes there's one, and then another, then another, right?" I used my hands to show this. "When those super hard words are stuck in the middle of your reading path, it's like you are in an obstacle course.

"You are running along, and everything is fine and dandy, and then, whoa! You come to a line of wobbly tires, and there is no way around them. You think, 'Should I give up? These look hard!' But readers don't let *anything* get in their way. Are you going to let those tires stop you? Are you going to let those tricky words stop you?

"No way! You rise to the challenge. You say, 'I can take on this hard word! I *love* a challenge.' You find a way to figure those words out so you can get through them and move on to the rest of the book."

❖ **Name the teaching point.**

"Today I want to teach you that when you want to get smart about your topic, you work at the hard words, even if they are long. One trick to reading long words is called 'crashing.' You can *crash* the parts of the word together and then think, 'What word makes sense here?'"

IN THIS SESSION, you'll teach children that one strategy readers use to figure out a tricky word is to "crash" the word parts together and then to check that the word makes sense. You will practice doing this by reading the beginning, middle, and end of the word and then putting the parts together to form a word.

GETTING READY

✔ Choose a couple of multisyllabic words from a text and spell out the words with magnetic letters on the board. Then cover the letters with strips of paper, and cover the same words in the book. We use *I Want to Be a Doctor*, by Dan Leibman (see Teaching and Active Engagement).

✔ Display the anchor chart "Good Habits for Solving Hard Words" so it is ready to refer to and extend (see Link and Mid-Workshop Teaching).

✔ Prepare today's strategy Post-it—"Crash the parts together."—to add to the chart (see Link).

✔ Choose a book to show to the class, possibly using the document camera, to model crashing words with a partner (see Transition to Partner Time).

✔ Prepare to add to a class book. We use *Our School* (see Share).

✔ Prepare to distribute white boards and markers for children to use to practice writing words (see Share).

TEACHING

Demonstrate the strategy of crashing word parts together to figure out hard words.

"Readers, put your two hands together and *crash* them!" I said while demonstrating, almost as if I had cymbals in each hand. The children tried it. Nodding, I said, "That is one of the ways that readers figure out tricky words. They look at the parts and crash them back together.

"I found another long hard word in the book about doctors that we have been reading," I told them. "I sucked the word right out of the book—*swoosh*—and put the letters on the board." I dramatically gestured from the covered word in the book to the board, where I had placed magnetic letters beneath a strip of paper. "*Swoosh!*" I exclaimed as I pulled away the strip of paper to show the row of letters.

e - x - e - r - c - i - s - i - n - g

"Okay, watch what I do next. First, I am going to get a running start in the book." I dramatically pointed in the book and read, 'This boy is . . .' Pretending to be stuck, I said, "Oh! This is a super long hard word." I turned to the magnetic letters. "To figure out that word, I am going to start pulling over the letters to make word parts that we know. I see an *e* and an *x*' Those two letters stay together, like in the word *example*." I slid over the two letters together and said it: /ex/. "Hmm, . . . Is this enough to help us read this word?" I asked and shook my head.

"We need more letters. Let's look at the next part." I slid together the *e* and the *r* and said, "/er/. "Now I am ready to crash this part together with the *ex*." To dramatize this, I held up one fist to represent *ex* and the other fist for *er* and said, "/exer/," while crashing the two fists together. "*Exer!* Is *exer* a word? Nope, not yet."

I gathered up three more letters—*c, i, s*—saying, "/cis/" with a short *i* sound, and I started reading the parts from left to right.

ex - er - cis -

Then I crashed the parts together: "/exercis/. Hmm, . . . Maybe I'll try it with a long *i* sound now." I read it again with a long *i* sound. "That sounds like the word *exercise*. But I haven't crashed everything together yet." I then put together the letters *i, n,* and *g*. I read from the beginning of the word, crashing each part together.

ex - er - cis - ing

"*Exercising*. That's a word!

"Did you see how we read left to right all the parts, gathering more and more parts each time to think about what the word could be? Even before we finished the word, some of you knew it!"

You are using the term crashing *parts of words together in this lesson to make it more memorable for the children, but you are actually teaching children about reading and blending parts together, critical phonics skills for young children to be able to do successfully and automatically as they progress as readers.*

This strategy helps students word solve more efficiently. Here they are asked to integrate the sources of information as they work on problem-solving the word.

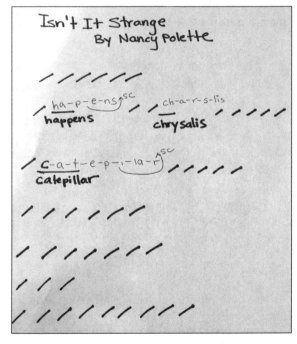

This reader could benefit from word solving with more efficiency. This reader, while she can fix up her errors (2/3), is still reading letter by letter, without crashing any of them along the way. You might teach a reader like this that, as they say the parts of the word, they could be thinking, "What could this word be? What would make sense?"

Reread the section of the book where the word appears, putting the word back into context and reading smoothly.

"But wait. We are not done crashing until we put the word back in the book." I tapped the magnetic letters that spelled *exercising* and, with a "Swoosh," tapped the book and peeled off the Post-it that had covered the word. "Let's read the whole sentence now that we have figured out this hard word and put it back in the book.

> This boy is exercising his legs to make the muscles grow strong again.

"Does *exercising* make sense, sound right, and look right? Yep! Let's read on to the next hard word in this book."

ACTIVE ENGAGEMENT

Recruit children to join you in solving the next hard word by crashing its parts together.

"Let's try crashing the next hard word we come across." I turned the page where I had covered the word *operation*. The magnetic letters were already on the board under another strip of paper.

"Ready to suck the hard word right out of the book and onto the board?" I asked, holding my hand over the covered word in the book. "All together, *swoosh*!" The children all swooshed their hands from the book to the board as I unveiled the magnetic letters.

o - p - e - r - a - t - i - o - n

"Now, the important thing to remember about crashing words is that you need to crash parts together, not just single letters. Look at the letters and decided which letters you are going to start with. Turn and tell your partner." I listened in to hear some of the ways the children were grouping the letters before I called them back together.

"I heard many of you say that you would start by putting the *o* and the *p* together, like in the word *open*." I slid the two letters together. "I'm going to add the *e* and the *r* to that. Read it with me: /oper/.

"Okay, tell your partner what letters you will put together next to crash into the /oper/ part here."

I listened briefly, then said, "I heard Jonah say he would put the *a* and the *t* together because that made a word that is on the word wall: *at*. Ready to crash the parts together? /operat/. Does that sound like a word? Not yet. Let's try a long vowel sound. /operate/. That's a word we know!"

Then as we looked at the last part of the word I said, "Oh, *tion* makes the /shun/ sound together."

op - er - a - tion

Not only do I crash the word parts together in the demonstration, I also check to make sure that the word I am saying makes sense in the book. Often, as students use this strategy, they will figure out words before they have crashed all the word parts together. This is fine and, in fact, welcomed. These students are integrating all the sources of information as they read.

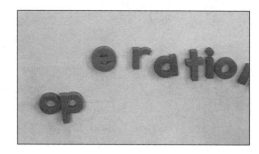

FIG. 8–1 Using magnetic letters, white boards, or other word study tools during reading workshop can help support students in transferring word study work into reading workshop.

"Let's crash the parts together! Start at the beginning of the word and crash all the parts together." We all read "operation." Then we *swooshed* the word back into the book.

"When you are reading your books, you always want to put the word back and reread the sentence to make sure it makes sense, sounds right, and looks right. Let's check all three of these things."

This man is having an operation on his wrist.

"Do you know what an operation is? Do people have operations on their bodies? Yes, so it makes sense, sounds right, and looks right! Way to go, readers!"

LINK

Reiterate the importance of trying everything you know to figure out a hard word, including today's strategy.

"Readers, you've got a baggie full of new books you started yesterday. When you go off to read, don't let long words be obstacles that stop you in your tracks. Remember, don't let anything stand in the way of learning as much as you can about your topics, especially a long word.

"If you are having a hard time checking to see if something makes sense and looks right, you might try *crashing* the parts of a word together. Each time you try to say the word, add a new part to the whole. Keep coming back to the beginning of the word as you add in those new parts until you hear the whole word smoothly together. And if you keep thinking to yourself, 'What could that word be?' you're likely to figure it out more quickly!"

I reviewed the anchor chart:

ANCHOR CHART

Good Habits for Solving Hard Words

- Check the picture.
- Look at ALL the parts of the word.
- Get a running start.
- Check it! Do a double-check!
- Try it 2 ways!
- **Crash the parts together.**

Crash the parts together.

You may have noticed that we went ahead and told the class that tion *says /shun/, knowing that most first-graders will not have learned that spelling pattern. The kids are invited to help solve the parts they'll be successful with, and the teacher solves the rest. This is a move you might make as well when doing this kind of word work together as a class. Another option would be to choose a different word, perhaps with fewer syllables or easier spelling patterns. Choose a word in which most of your class will recognize familiar spelling patterns so they can successfully break the word into parts.*

Good Habits for Solving Hard Words

Check the Picture.

Look at ALL the parts of the word.

Get a running start.

Check it! Do a double-check!

Try it 2 ways.

Crash the parts together.

Supporting Readers in Various Ways and Moving Them toward Independence

Use shared reading and guided reading to introduce new and challenging texts to small groups of children.

Today, like yesterday, you'll presumably divide your time between conferring and small-group work, and you'll probably lead a variety of small groups. For example, with one small group of kids, you may support some shared reading, using that shared reading as a pipeline to provide each of those group members with more books to try reading independently. You might convene a small group to support kids' seeing more on a page, thinking more about each page, and relating the content of that one page to the content of the whole book. Presumably, if you began a guided reading group yesterday, you'll return to that group either today or tomorrow. As you think about a second session with that same guided reading group, begin to consider ways to lighten your scaffolding for the students and move them toward reading this level with more independence.

(continues)

MID-WORKSHOP TEACHING   **Being Flexible with Vowels**

"Readers, it's exciting watching you rise to the challenge of solving the longer words in your books. Figuring out a word is fun, right? Don't get frustrated, though, if your first try doesn't work. Anytime you try to conquer something new, it can take a few tries.

"Some of you have been running into the same problem we all ran into together when we tried to solve the words *exercising* and *operation*. Sometimes when you try to crash the sounds of a hard word together, the parts don't sound right. This might be because you've made the vowels into a short vowel sound when they should be a long vowel sound—or vice versa!

"If you try to read a hard word, crashing the parts together, and you try to say the sounds using short vowels and it *still* doesn't sound like a word you know, try solving it again, *this time* using long vowel sounds. See if that makes the word sound like one that would fit.

"Remember, readers can try it two ways!" I gestured toward the chart, reminding students of the strategy they had learned in the previous unit. "Trying out different vowel sounds and thinking about different possibilities will help you figure out those hard words.

"Keep reading and keep rising to the challenges that come up in your books. And if one thing doesn't work, try something else!"

I reminded students once more to use the word-solving strategy chart whenever they need it:

> **ANCHOR CHART**
>
> Good Habits for Solving Hard Words
> - Check the picture.
> - Look at ALL the parts of the word.
> - Get a running start.
> - Check it! Do a double-check!
> - Try it 2 ways!
> - Crash the parts together.

TRANSITION TO PARTNER TIME
Reading New and Challenging Books with Partner Support

"Readers, it's time to read with your partners. As you stack up your books, getting ready to read with your partners, put the books that you haven't read yet from your book bins at the top as the first books to read with your partner. Remember to be the kind of reader who reads all of your books.

"Also, because your partner is a great helper, it is wise to read the books that you don't yet know well together. That will help you with reading those books on your own tomorrow and the next day. As you and your partner read and encounter obstacles, you can help each other tackle those challenges."

I projected a book using the document camera. "To help you and your partner read and crash a word, you can use your finger to cover up parts of the word and slowly reveal new parts like this." I gave a quick demonstration.

"Go ahead and start reading through your stack of books with your partner. Remember to be good helpers!"

You might decide to adapt this transition to provide just one tip, rather than two, as students switch to partner time. In most classrooms, though, kids will easily grasp both suggestions because each relates to familiar reading work that has already been taught in previous minilessons.

You may decide to do a brief book introduction where you *mostly* support the comprehension of the text. To prepare for this introduction, you might think of it as providing kids with a paragraph of information about the book. It's also helpful to remind students of the instruction you gave them on the preceding day. Then, most importantly, give the book to your students to read. As they read, cycle among them, coaching them with lean prompts. As students reach the end of the book, you can channel them to talk in partnerships or in the whole group about the content of the book. Then you can offer one tip, one teaching point, suggesting to students that this is something they can practice using both the new book they'll have read that day and also the book they read during the previous guided reading session.

Remember to observe what your students do at the point of error, and, if necessary, to prompt them to check themselves. Prompt readers also whenever they seem unsure of what they are reading, when they appeal to you for answers, and when they read words as questions and look at you for reassurance. They may *not* have made an error, but you don't want to be the one who conveys that to them. Instead, to help build more self-reliance and confidence in your readers, prompt them to check for themselves. You might say, "You are wondering if it says /football/? You aren't sure? Then go back, reread, and check it! Make sure it looks right and makes sense." Or you might prompt readers, "You sound like you are not sure. Look at the word. Reread and check it." It is important that you ask for that checking even when students have read correctly, because you are teaching them to cross-check with meaning, to ask, "Does that make sense?" If students discover that no, the word they produced was not correct, then of course, they will need to access their fix-up strategies.

Use word sorts from phonics work to give students more support and practice using those features when they read.

You may decide to pull a small group of readers who are reading below benchmark and who need extra support in phonics. For example, you might bring together a small group of readers who need support with short vowel sounds. Have them bring some word sorts that they have been studying in word study time and do a couple of speed sorts with short vowel sounds with a partner. Coach students to check their sorts with the anchor words. Leave out the sorts that they finish. Ask students to take out their books and read them and retell them with a partner. Then have partners search and find other words that have the short vowel sounds that match their sorts. Have them then write those words down on Post-its and add them to their sorts. Have them do another speed sort with their new words added.

Using materials from word study time—magnetic letters, sorts, making and breaking words, and even word walls—is a great way to practice and warm up before reading. It is also a nice way to make links between the word work students do in isolation with that which they are doing in context.

Solving Hard Words in Writing, Too

Engage kids in shared writing with a focus on thinking about word parts and how they sound.

"Readers, you have been looking closely at the words in your books and reading the parts of the words, all the while thinking about what would make sense. You do the same thing as you write. You think about the parts of the word and the sounds of each part, and you spell the best you can.

"Let's write a chapter about gym in our class book, *Our School*. Let's first think about what you want to say, and then let's write it together.

"What should we teach first about gym? Turn and talk with your partners." I circulated, coaching some kids talking about what they thought we could teach, and then brought the group back together, "We can teach people about the games that we play in gym. So, we could say, 'We are learning how to play different games in gym class.' Let's write that together. I'll write some, and you'll write some." I said and wrote:

> We are

When it was time to write *learning*, I asked for students' help. I said, "Okay, take out your white boards and take the caps off your markers. Try listening to the parts of the word: /l/er/n/ing. "Four parts! Carla, come on up and write it, and the rest of you, write it on your white boards." As Carla came up to the chart paper, the students worked, and I voiced over to coach all of them. "Say the word again and think, 'What sounds do I hear? What spelling patterns can I use?'" Carla easily wrote "l," as did the rest of the class. "Say the next part of the word. What spelling patterns do we know that could help us?"

"/l/er/ . . . e-r!" said Carla. We had been sorting *-er*, *-ir*, and *-or* words earlier that week. I chimed in that in *learn* the /er/ part was spelled yet another new way, *ear*, like in the words *earn*, *earth*, and *search*. "*Learn* is just one of those oddball words with a funny spelling! Now you know. Go ahead and write that part." A bit later I said, "Listen to the ending. It's an ending we have been studying. There are three letters that make up the ending."

As Carla and other students finished, I said, "Caps on! Hold up your boards! Check your word with Carla's! Now erase. Boards down. Let's reread and think about what word comes next." We finished the sentence in the same manner. Students interacted with two more words before moving on to a second sentence. "Wow, you have really built up your reading and writing muscle power now! You used to write letter by letter, listening for just one little sound at a time. But now you have awesome reading and writing muscles, and you can listen for and write whole parts of a word."

FIG. 8–2 This is an example of a shared writing text that another first-grade class wrote together. You'll notice the ways in which that class used writing strategies to elaborate on ideas and features to help them organize and teach the information.

Readers Check that the Words They Read Look Right and Make Sense

MINILESSON

In the connection, let students know that the work they did yesterday is not only helping them get through longer and harder words, but it is also helping them learn more about the world. Congratulate your students for being the kind of readers who enjoy the challenge of working through the hard parts and not being stopped by anything in their books.

To set your students up for today's teaching point, describe how slowing down and making a careful check is just as important as powering through something difficult. You could return to the metaphor of this bend, saying, "In an obstacle course, not only do you use all your muscles to power through, but you also have to be careful where you place your foot and check that your grip is just right." Then tell them that readers do the same thing; not only do they power through words; they also do a slow check. You could say, "Readers are always on the lookout for obstacles and tricky words to make sure that what they read is what is *actually* on the page."

Name the teaching point by saying something like, "Today I want to teach you that sometimes when you ask, 'Does it look right?' you might need to do a *slow check*. In the same way you say a word slowly to spell it, you can run your finger under the word and say it slowly to check if it looks right. Then you can reread to double-check that the word makes sense."

Add today's strategy Post-it, "Do a *slow* check!," to the anchor chart "Good Habits for Solving Hard Words."

During your teaching, select a text to project with the document camera for students to see and read with you. Begin to read a small portion of the text, and *purposefully* misread a word. Say to the class, "Wait, wait! That doesn't look right! Does it? I think it needs a *slow* check. I'll put my finger under the word, and let's say it slowly and check if it looks right."

Afterward, remind students to reread. You might say something like, "Let's go back and smooth out our reading. Let's also check that it makes sense." Then reread the text together as a class, and point out to students how the slow check helped everyone read the word that was on the page—and also check that it made sense. You could say to them, "You made it through yet another challenge. What fun! Now we can learn the information that the author wants us to learn! Now we can get back to learning about the world."

> **Good Habits for Solving Hard Words**
>
> - Check the picture.
> - Look at ALL the parts of the word.
> - Get a running start.
> - Check it! Do a double-check!
> - Try it 2 ways!
> - Crash the parts together.
> - **Do a <u>slow</u> check!**

During the active engagement, choose another excerpt from the same text and have students read it on their own. Select a word that you think they may not be able to read on their own or that they may misread. Whether they make an error or not, raise the question, "Did that look right? Let's do a *slow check*. I'll slide my finger underneath, and you all read! Now let's reread and double-check that it makes sense, too."

In the link, restate what you taught children today, and remind them when they should use what they learned. You might say to them, "Don't wait for the word to tell you *this is hard*. *You* be on the lookout for what is hard or what might trip you up. Remember, a slow check is a great way to double-check that what you are reading is, in fact, what is written on the page."

You might then point to the anchor chart that you have been using in this bend and say, "Now you have a new way to make sure that what you read looks right and makes sense! Let's reread our chart to remember *all* the things that readers can do to help them through challenges and obstacles they find in books."

CONFERRING AND SMALL-GROUP WORK

As you begin to circulate and pull small groups today, remember to do two things. First, confer with students and support them with word solving as they confront hard words in their texts. Second, steer your guided reading groups toward reading at the next text level more independently.

You might begin by conducting a couple of conferences. Try asking students a few questions as they read, such as "How many times have you read this book? What are you hoping to learn? What will you do when you finish the book? What does that mean?" Observe and listen to your students read. Notice how fluent their reading is and what they do when confronted with challenges. Newer books in their baggies will likely present more challenges than books they have reread multiple times. After you have listened and asked a few questions, pick a teaching point. You may decide to coach a reader through long, hard words, helping him make use of meaning, structure, and visual sources of information in the text (MSV) as he reads. Or you may decide to help him slow down and see more on the page. Whatever you decide to teach, don't just remind readers what to do; also ask them to practice something a few times in their books while you give them feedback. Then remind them, "You can do this throughout this book, and in all of your other books, too."

Next, you might decide to pull the guided reading group you started a couple days ago for a second or third day. Try to lighten a few scaffolds to help students move to the next level with more independence.

During this guided reading group, you may want your students to work in partnerships to set themselves up to read. Coach students to give themselves a sneak peek, their own book introduction. Have them study the title and the cover, glance at the back cover to see if there is any information there, and walk through some of the pictures at the beginning of the book. To help release the scaffolding you've been providing and encourage kids to work independently, use minimal coaching, giving reminders only when needed.

Instead of reading alone or to you during guided reading, you might have students begin to read with their partners like a seesaw, one reading one page, and the other reading the next page. Ask students to coach one another through the reading. This allows children to verbalize the strategies you have been prompting for; instead of you always being the one saying all the prompts, now they are doing it themselves.

Near the end, it's important to have a brief discussion about the text. You might ask students to retell, across their fingers, what the book was mostly about. Then give your readers a teaching point. Teach them something that you frequently prompted them for as they were partner reading. You might say, "One thing to do as readers is remember to say the first part of the word and think about what would make sense. Say a short vowel sound, and then try a long vowel sound. This may help you figure out the word."

Give each of the students a copy of the text so that they can read it on their own. If you have a minute or so left in your small group, listen to them and coach them to reread the text with you. If not, leave students to read on their own and put the new book in their baggie.

Mid-Workshop Teaching

You might want to remind your readers that not only can they slow-check to make sure something *looks right*, but they can also double-check to make sure that something *makes sense*. You might say, "Readers, I've noticed that sometimes when you read a word, you aren't double-checking that it makes sense. Then

This reader tries to say something for every word. She tries to fix her errors about half of the time. When this reader says a "word," using some of the letters, she does not cross-check with meaning or language structure, and never goes back to reread, to make sure that whatever word she has said fits with the whole. Rereading after a reader has figured out a word is a good habit to develop. This lesson will help students cross-check as they read, integrate the sources of information, and make rereading a habit.

when you get further in the book, you don't understand the information you're reading. You've read all the words, but you forgot to double-check by asking, 'Does that make sense?'"

Tell them that to double-check, they can think about how what they just read fits with what they have learned from the book so far. Tell them they can also make pictures in their minds using all the words to make sure it all goes together. Then they should be able to verify that it makes sense.

You may ask them to give this a quick try with the page they are reading. Ask them to double-check that what they read made sense. Ask them prove it to a partner and then have them continue reading. Say to them, "Keep reading and keep being on the lookout for obstacles, before they become too big!"

Transition to Partner Time

Partners can help one another by being on the lookout for challenges and by reminding each other of things to try. Remind your readers that they are helpers, not just when parts seem difficult or when they seem like a challenge, but also before things get too hard! Say to your readers, "As you listen to one another read, if you hear your partner read something that makes sense *and* looks right, tell her. Give her a little thumbs up! If something looks fishy or sounds fishy, don't forget to say, 'Check it!' Maybe you can help your partner do a slow check or double-check that what she read makes sense with the rest of the book."

SHARE

Celebrate several readers and what they figured out in their books. Invite the first reader to join you, book in hand, at the front of the meeting area, and say, "When Jennifer was reading, she encountered a challenge! You got stuck on which word, Jennifer? This word," and point to it. "And what did you do to figure it out?" Make sure your anchor chart is on display so that the student you've called forward can use it and recall any strategies that helped her. Then you might say, "Let's reread this part with Jennifer, doing what she did!" Lead a short whole-class shared reading with Jennifer's book. Then say to kids, "Give Jennifer a big fist bump in the sky for using all her reading strength to power through that word. Now Marcos is going to share what he did."

Readers Learn New Words as They Read

IN THIS SESSION, you'll teach children that some tricky words are new words. Readers solve these tricky words by saying the word the best they can and then thinking about what that word means.

GETTING READY

✔ Mask two or three domain-specific vocabulary words in a nonfiction text. We return to *I Want to Be a Doctor*, by Dan Leibman. Prepare to project the pages with the covered words, perhaps using the document camera (see Teaching and Active Engagement).

✔ Display the anchor chart "Good Habits for Solving Hard Words" so it is ready to refer to and extend (see Link).

✔ Prepare the strategy Post-it—"Say the word the best you can. Think about what it means."—to add to the chart (see Link).

✔ Prepare a partner vocabulary game by writing on Post-it notes several words from a student's book or one from the classroom library. Plan a few clues that gradually become more specific for two or three of the words (see Share).

✔ Display the diagram page and word list page in *Hang On, Monkey!* under the document camera (see Mid-Workshop Teaching).

MINILESSON

CONNECTION

Celebrate students' perseverance in tackling tricky words, and encourage them to keep working through unfamiliar vocabulary.

"Readers, you are working hard at using *all* that you know to rise to the challenge of reading harder and longer words. These obstacles really take a lot of muscles to get through. You know that to become as smart as you can about your topics, you can't let these things stop you.

"Some of you are finding a new obstacle with words in your books. You are bumping into words that you have not heard before. You may not really be sure what they mean. I want you to know that all readers, at some point, have encountered this very same thing. It isn't a bad thing. It's actually a great thing, because it means that you get another chance to get smarter! You get to add more words to what you already know about the world!

"Books will teach you new words about your topics. When you learn new words, you will be able to use them when you talk to people like your partners, me, and your friends and family. As you read, make sure that you don't *ignore* these kinds of words. Be sure to *figure out* these words as well!"

❖ **Name the teaching point.**

"Today I want to teach you that when readers run into a *new* word, they don't ignore those words, nor do they let those words stop them from reading and learning about their topic. They say the word the *best* that they can and think, 'What does this new word mean?'"

TEACHING AND ACTIVE ENGAGEMENT

Guide students to use pictures and context clues to figure out the meaning of unknown words.

"Let's try it together. I have covered up two words on this page. You are going to try to say a lot of things about what you think these words might mean.

"Are you ready to try? Let's read another part of our doctor book.

If you break a bone, the doctor puts on a _____.

"Now, let's use as many words as we can to describe what this word might mean. Let's not let anything stop us. With your partner, try to say what you think the word might mean, what might this be in the picture, what the thing that this word refers to might look like, what it might do." I paused, giving kids a chance to think. "Go ahead, turn and talk."

After students had a chance to talk, I said, "Readers, listen up. I heard things like, 'It is this white thing on her arm,' and 'It is long.' Someone else said, 'It looks like a big bandage. It is helping her arm.' Do you see how, without knowing exactly what the word is, you are already learning a lot about what this word probably means?

"I am going to uncover the word. Let's pronounce it the *best* we can."

If you break a bone, the doctor puts on a cast . . .

"I knew it! I had a cast once!" Renee shouted.

"Well, now, let's explain to each other again, this time using the word, what it *means*. A cast means . . . The cast helps you . . . A cast looks like . . . Turn and use as many words as you can to talk about the *new* word *cast*."

Try it again.

"Let's work on the second word. Ready to reread? Remember, let's think about what this word might mean."

If you break a bone, the doctor puts on a cast until the bone _____.

"Turn and talk. Say as much as you can about what you think this word may mean." After we talked about the word a bit, we uncovered it and then reread the whole sentence. Then, students talked about what the word *heals* means.

You will want your students to know that when they are reading nonfiction texts they can expect to learn new and important words. As the texts they read become more complex, so too does the vocabulary that they will encounter. Some texts they read will be more supportive than others.

Asking the kids to talk about the word using as many words as they can is a way to help them generate synonyms and use the new word in a meaningful conversation. Some students may talk about examples, while others may be able to describe the word. In any case, the goal is to support students in understanding what the word means. Here, students are building context for the word, not just stating a definition. This is much more effective than only seeing the word in print or hearing the teacher say the word. Students will be encountering more and more words that they are expected to learn through reading. These strategies will help students begin to do that work.

You may have noticed that neither word (cast nor heals) is particularly difficult to decode, but both could be challenging in terms of meaning. You will want to select similar types of words for this lesson.

LINK

Encourage students to work with their partners to figure out the meanings of new words.

"Words are fun to think about. Even though it may feel like a challenge, challenges can be fun too! Here's the really great thing. Thinking about words can help you learn even more! Just because something is a little bit hard or tricky, that doesn't mean it should stop us, does it?! Obstacle courses are fun, and learning new words is fun, too.

"As you are reading on in your books and rereading them, check to see what *new* words you could be thinking *more* about. Don't ignore those new words! Think about what they might mean. Then, when you get together with your partner today, see if your partner knows that word. Together, the two of you can think and talk even more about the new words."

I added the new strategy Post-it note to the chart:

ANCHOR CHART

Good Habits for Solving Hard Words

- Check the picture.
- Look at ALL the parts of the word.
- Get a running start.
- Check it! Do a double-check!
- Try it 2 ways!
- Crash the parts together.
- Do a <u>slow</u> check!
- **Say the word the best you can.**
  Think about what it means.

Say the word the best you can.

Think about what it means.

Supporting the Learning of New Vocabulary

Assess how students are working to understand what they are reading.

This is a good time to assess students' reading and thinking about their books. As you confer with readers, open up some research by asking a few questions. You might begin, "What is this book teaching you?" or "Tell me a lot about what you're learning and thinking about here, as you read this book." Then, ask the student to read to you. You might ask how the student is addressing the information and vocabulary he encounters, saying, "What does that mean? Can you explain that word to me?"

MID-WORKSHOP TEACHING
Using Diagrams to Learn New Words

From the middle of the classroom, I used our class quiet signal to call for kids' attention and said, "Readers, as you are thinking about *new* important words in your books, other things may help you think about what these words mean. Some of your books might have diagrams and picture word lists, like in *Hang On, Monkey!*" I showed an example with the document camera. "Marco also found one in his book, *Busy Tractors, Busy Days*, by Lori Houran." I then projected the relevant page from his book. "You also might have one. If you do, don't skip it! Use it to help you learn new words and know what is important about your topic.

"Be sure to use those tools as you read to help you learn and think about what the *new* words mean!"

This is just as true when you are reading aloud nonfiction to your kids. In most cases, you won't want to skip the table of contents, diagrams, word lists, and other features (there may be exceptions, of course). Read these features aloud and discuss them just as you would all the other parts of the book.

Listen carefully to the reader, and then name something the reader is doing that will be helpful to continue. You might say, "I like the way you stopped on that page and studied the picture to help you think about what the word means. That's a good thing to do a lot as you read. Especially when there is a new word!"

Then, steer the conference toward a teaching point. Alert the reader that you are ready to teach. You might say, "I want to teach you one thing that can help when . . ."

You may also want to pull some small groups in which you coach readers to be better partners. Pull two or three partnerships together and say to them, "You know that partners don't just help each other tackle tricky words. They also make sure to think while they are *listening* to each other read—to get ready to help out. Our chart can help you remember the types of thinking you might do. After you hear your partner read, don't forget to add your thinking. Choose something on the chart to do to push yourself to think!"

TRANSITION TO PARTNER TIME
Figuring Out New Words Together

"Time for partner reading. As you are studying together, make sure you help each other study and talk about as much as you can. If there is a word that *either* of you doesn't know or isn't sure of, try to figure it out together.

"Ask each other, 'What does _____ mean? How do you know?' or 'Can you explain what that means? I don't understand.' If you stop each other this way, you will *both* end up much smarter about a topic. You will have taught someone else and probably learned a new word to use, not only in this book, but in your life!"

Playing a Game to Learn New Words

Recruit students to play a game with their new vocabulary.

"Readers, you have been getting through so many difficult obstacles, and I thought we should play a game with the new words we are learning!

"I chose some of Natalie's words from her book. I have them in front of me on these Post-it notes. I am going to talk about the word that I have on this Post-it note first, *but* I am not going to say the word. *You* are going to have to guess the word! Let's try and play together! Are you ready? As soon as you think you know the word, put your thumb on your knee.

"The word I am thinking about is a part of the elephant's body. Oh, already some people think they know what it is. I am going to give some more clues, so make sure it still fits with what you think. It is long, wrinkled, and gray. Elephants use it like an arm. What word is it? Whisper it to your partner. What do you think? *Trunk*. Exactly." We played with a couple more words together, and then partners played with each other.

"Partner 1, give clues about one of your words and let Partner 2 try to guess it. And then we will switch. Give your partner lots and lots of clues, but don't say the word.

"Learning *new* words is like bumping into new obstacles on a course, but it can be just as fun as that game! I am sure you will learn more and more words, because you are the kind of readers who try to get smarter and smarter about your topics."

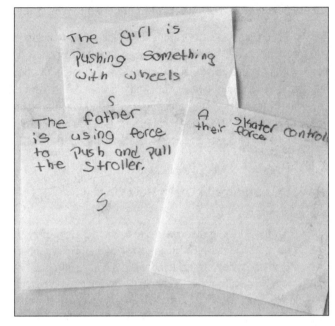

FIG. 10–1 One student's ideas as she studied a book on forces and motion

Readers Find and Think about Key Words

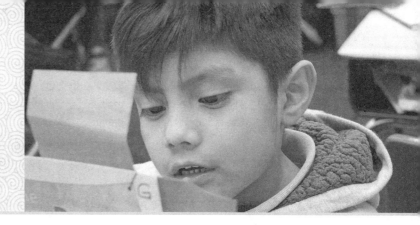

IN THIS SESSION, you'll teach students that key words can help readers think and talk about the information in their books.

MINILESSON

CONNECTION

Introduce students to owning key words about their topics.

"Readers, who knew that baby cows and whales were called *calves*? Whoa! And who knew that to fly a plane you hold a *yoke*? Wow! And who knew that a fox's home was called a *den*? Yes! You've been learning so many interesting things about the world, and along the way, you are learning *new* words. Those words are teaching you *so* many cool things. You aren't letting anything get in your way of becoming smarter about your topics.

"As you read nonfiction, you become an expert on a topic, and becoming an expert means getting to know (even to *own*) the key words related to the topic. Each one of you is an expert already on things you know from your life. Is there someone here who is an expert on soccer? Stand up and take a bow." The class soccer fanatics took bows. "I thought so. I'm pretty sure you know a whole *bunch* of soccer words. Am I right?" They started to list soccer words, until I quieted them and continued.

"This is my point. Whenever you are learning about a topic, there are *key words* that are super important to that topic. So if a person wanted to learn about reading workshop, one key word would be *minilessons*, and another key word would be . . ." and I pointed to the shelves, "*books*. Learning about a topic means learning about the key words related to that topic."

GETTING READY

✔ Select a few key words that are important to the topic from any nonfiction book, and have several blank Post-it notes ready for writing down key words. We use *I Want to Be a Doctor*, by Dan Liebman (see Teaching and Active Engagement and Mid-Workshop Teaching).

✔ Display the anchor chart "How to Get Super Smart about Nonfiction Topics" so it is ready to refer to and extend (see Link, Conferring and Small-Group Work, and Mid-Workshop Teaching).

✔ Prepare the strategy Post-it—"Find and think about key words."—to add to the chart (see Link).

✔ Place Post-it notes at tables for students to record key words from their books (see Link).

✔ Write key words from a demonstration text on index cards and display them in a pocket chart. We use key words from *Hang On, Monkey!*, by Susan B. Neuman (see Share).

✔ Distribute index cards to children for collecting and trading key words from their books (see Share).

❖ Name the teaching point.

"Today I want to teach you that it is important to be on the lookout for *key words*, words that are key to understanding your topic. It's like these words unlock knowledge." I mimed turning a key. "When you find a key word, try extra hard not just to read that word and say that word, but to *own* that word."

TEACHING

Demonstrate using a key word multiple times to really own the word.

"Let's read the next few pages in our doctor book, and let's look out for some key words. Then let's not just *read* them. Let's *own* them."

> *Patients sometimes have to be very brave. This girl needs oxygen to help her.*

"First, we need to figure out what key words there are here. I think *patients* is a key word, because they are really important people to doctors. Show me a thumb on your knee if you agree. I am just going to jot that down here, on a Post-it note.

"Now *patients* is *not* a new word for me, but I still want to *own* it. Let's think about what we know and are learning about patients in our book about doctors.

"Let me say one thing about the key word. Doctors help patients. True, right? Look at the doctor helping this patient breathe."

Each time I said *patient*, I pointed to the word on the Post-it note.

"Let me ask a question about patients: Are patients always sick? I know I am not *always* sick when I go to the doctor. Sometimes I just get a check-up. Like . . ." I flipped the pages back to the page which showed a baby getting what appeared to be a well-baby check-up. "This baby is getting a check-up, so this patient isn't sick. Sometimes, though, patients are *very* sick, like this little girl who needs oxygen.

"As we keep reading this book, we can think even *more* about this key word, *patients*, and learn more and more about it."

Debrief what you taught and name the steps of the strategy that you used.

"Did you see, here, I chose a key word to pay attention to? Then I thought about the word and thought more about the topic! Did you hear how many times I said the word, *patient*? I really started to *own* it."

FIG. 11–1 When asked why she chose these words, the student said, "These are all important to trucks. Trucks load things like dirt and rocks into other trucks like a backhoe. Trucks carry them places. Like cranes carry things too. And cement trucks carry . . . cement!"

ACTIVE ENGAGEMENT

Invite students to identify other key words related to the topic. Then choose one and ask students to use it in their partner talk.

"Let's read on and find another key word that will help us think about our topic more.

> *This doctor carefully scrubs his hands before touching the patient. It is important that germs do not spread from one to another and another in the hospital.*

"Let's first pick a word. Whisper quickly to your partner. What word do you think is a key word to know about doctors?

"*Patients* is one that we already know. I heard some kids say *germs* is a good key word, because that's the thing that causes patients to get sick. Let's write that on our Post-it note.

"Now you can try to say something about the word and how it teaches us about doctors. You can also ask questions. We will try and use the word as much as we can, so that we can *own* it. Let's read this page one more time and then talk to our partners." We reread the page together, and then students discussed germs with their partners.

"I heard kids saying things like, 'Even doctors sometimes have germs,' and 'Germs make people, like patients, sick.' I heard, 'Doctors have to wash the germs away so that they don't get their patients sick,' and 'Where do the germs come from?'

"You are not only starting to *own* the key words *germs* and *patients*, but you are also really getting smarter about doctors!"

LINK

Remind students to think about the key words in their books, both new and familiar.

"As you go off to read, you can think about the key words in *your* books. You all have Post-it notes at your tables to help you start noting your key words.

Keywords not only help students understand the information in their books, they also help them retell and teach that information.

In some classrooms, teachers provide a special tool for collecting key words—a key word ring! You might staple or tie together four or five slips of paper or card stock, with a picture or outline of a key on each card. Alternatively, you might provide a key-themed sheet on which kids can collect key words as a handy tool for thinking and talking about their books. Post-its work just fine as well.

"Finding and thinking about key words will help you be ready for the challenges in your books. Sometimes, these words will be words that you know, and sometimes they will be *new* words. What's most important is that you are thinking about your topic and learning as much as you can. The more we know, the stronger we are, the better prepared we are for any challenge ahead! Remember, don't let anything stop you: long words, new words, or sloppy reading. Paying close attention to the pictures *and* the words on the page helps you become smarter about your topics."

I added the new strategy Post-it note to the anchor chart:

ANCHOR CHART

How to Get Super Smart
about Nonfiction Topics

- Take a sneak peek to start learning.
- Stop and study each page.
- Guess what might come next.
- Chat about a page or the book.
- Make your voice sound smooth & lively.
- **Find and think about key words.**

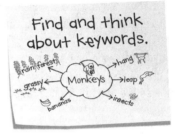

Using Charts as Tools

Gather students for strategy lessons based on informal assessments.

Today, as you confer and pull some small groups, assess whether students are doing the things you have listed on your "How to Get Super Smart about Nonfiction Topics" chart. Take a couple of minutes to observe your readers. Look to see which kids would benefit from lingering on the page more, which kids are not rereading, and which kids don't pause to consider the new words they should be learning.

You may want to gather together a few children who may be at different reading levels but who need similar reminders. Say to them, "Readers, I gathered you together because I've noticed that as you read, you do a sneak peek and you read all the words in your books. But I also notice that you haven't been doing these two things." Point to the items on the chart and say, "It seems you are forgetting to study the page and to guess what is going to happen next. Those are really important things to do when you read information books.

"Right now, will you reread the books in your stack and practice this? Make it your goal to learn even more information! I'll help you by reminding you to stop and think. When you get to the end of your book, check our chart and make sure you have tried these things."

(continues)

MID-WORKSHOP TEACHING   **Rereading with a Key Word in Mind**

"Readers, can I have your eyes up here, on me? As you are reading and learning about your topics, I know that you're not letting anything stand in your way! Meanwhile, I want to remind you that rereading can help you think more about your topic.

"When you reread, you can do *any* of the things on our chart, 'How to Get Super Smart about Nonfiction Topics.' You can also reread your book with a key word in mind and think, 'How do the pages in my book connect to this word?'

"So, I could reread our doctor book and think, 'How does each page connect to the key word *patient*?' Then I could reread again and think, 'How does each page connect to the word *germs*?' I can say what I think. I can even ask questions about it!

"Try this now with just one book that you've already read. Look at the stack of books you have finished. Choose one. Look at your key words. Pick a word that you think will help you reread and think more about your topic. Think about how that word connects to the different pages in your book. Then go on and read more. Continue stacking up your books!"

I reminded students to use the strategies on the anchor chart as they read:

ANCHOR CHART

How to Get Super Smart about Nonfiction Topics

- Take a sneak peek to start learning.
- Stop and study each page.
- Guess what might come next.
- Chat about a page or the book.
- Make your voice sound smooth & lively.
- Find and think about key words.

TRANSITION TO PARTNER TIME
Thinking about Key Words while Reading

> "Readers, it's partner time. Take out your books and get ready to stack them. Decide *how* you will read. Partner 2 will go first. *Before* you read today, take out your key words and show them to Partner 1.
>
> "Partner 2, Give Partner 1 a little introduction to what your book is about by showing him or her what key words are in your book and how they make you smarter about your topic. Then, as you two read, you can *both* be thinking and talking about the key words and information about your topics!
>
> "When you are done, switch roles. Keep reading. Try to read as many books in your stack as you can."

Gather small groups to practice shared reading together to work on a variety of foundational skills.

You may want to initiate a series of small groups throughout the week for below-benchmark-level students, using shared reading as the main method of instruction. On the first day, you could warm the group up with a shared reading text you have been using with the class. Share the pointer with your students by sometimes letting them hold it and point to the words to reinforce one-to-one matching and attending to the print. As you and the students read this text, you may pause a few times to ask students to find certain words, especially high-frequency words or words that exemplify a phonics feature that children are studying in word work time. Read the text together as a choral reading. Pick a couple of places to reinforce reading with more expression and scooping up more words at one time.

Then, introduce a new text to the group, just like you would to your whole class. Choose a text that is at a slightly higher level than the ones they are reading. For example, if they are level D readers, choose a level F text. After introducing the text, you might reread portions together, find high-frequency words, or play Guess the Covered Word with three or four words in the text.

Send kids off to read the newly introduced text in partnerships and independently.

At the end of the session, give each partnership a copy of the text to read together. Coach readers to help each other get through the text. When they're done reading, have them retell what the book was about. Then, give students copies of the book for their book baggies, so they can continue reading it for the rest of reading time and at home. In the next session, you'll find a description of what you might do with this group to lead them in reading a more complex text.

Comparing and Contrasting Key Words across Books

Guide children to match important key words from the text to important ideas in that text and other texts.

"You are becoming so super smart about the world! The cool thing about key words from *one* book is that often they make you think, 'Oh, hey, wait, that word is important to *this* book, too!' Here are some key words from *Hang On, Monkey!*" I fanned out several index cards on which I had written words pulled from the text. I placed each in a pocket chart as I read them aloud:

hang

leap

rain forest

grassy

bananas

insects

"See if any of these words make you think, 'Oh, hey, wait, that word is important to my book, too!' If you find one, reread to your partner the part of your book where it's mentioned. I will point to the word, and then you can search and think if it matches anything in your book." I gave children time to do this. "Thumbs up if you think you can use some of these key words to talk about your books and topics!" Several children indicated they could. I called one child up to try.

"Emilia, come up and take the key word you'll talk about," I invited, encouraging her to pull the word from the pocket chart.

"Hang," Emilia replied, taking it from the chart. I motioned for her to teach, using the key word. "Just like monkeys, bats hang upside down, but they don't leap."

"Oh! *another* key word. Quick, grab it!" I urged, as she took another card from the chart. "Keep going!"

FIG. 11–2   Zoe approximates her understanding of this new word. Now the teacher can give her feedback on the vocabulary work she has begun.

"Umm. I'm not sure if they live in the rain forest, but they do live in trees in some sort of forest!" I picked up *rain forest* from the chart and handed it to Emilia.

"Wow that's *three* key words to use when talking about bats! Who else is ready to give it a try?" I called another student up, placing the three index cards back into the pocket chart.

Carl came up, quickly grabbing *grassy* and *rain forest*. "My book is about race cars, and sometimes they race on tracks in grassy places." He held up the word, *grassy*. "But they definitely don't race in rain forests because there are too many trees. They race on concrete."

"Oh! That's a key word we can add—*concrete*." I quickly took a blank index card and recorded the word, handing it to Carl. "You see, we can borrow each other's key words, knowing they may make us think more about our own topics, even when they don't fit perfectly! Even Carl started thinking about the place where cars race, because we read about *places* in *Hang On, Monkey!*"

Teach children to pull out important key words to use in discussing the book with their partners.

"Guess what! You can write down some of the key words from *your* books and talk about them. Then, you can trade them with your partner, so your partner can try to use them, too. I'm going to hand each of you two index cards. Quickly, write a key word on each. Then, take turns using them to talk. Then, make a trade, and use your partner's key words to talk about your book. Ready? Go!"

FIG. 11–3 "Mathew didn't know what yolk meant. You can see his approximated understanding of the word. This is an opportunity to give students feedback, not just about what the word means, but on their attempts to think about a new word.

Rereading a Page to Find the Just-Right Sound

MINILESSON

In the connection, you might tell students that when they overcome an obstacle or figure out a hard word in a book, the last thing they should remember to do—always—is reread. Tell them that rereading is important not just to smooth out their voices, but also to hear and show what, in their books, is important. This will help them learn and hold onto more information.

You could then show a short video clip about a nonfiction topic. For example, you might use a clip from the PBS program *Wild Kratts*, a nature show narrated by the two zoologist Kratt brothers. Show a short clip of the brothers talking to the audience, and then say, "This is not just a fun show to watch. It's a show that teaches people a lot about the world! Watching a show like this is similar to reading books. When you are reading, try to make your voice sound like the voices in a show like this one."

Name the teaching point by saying something like, "Today I want to teach you that readers of nonfiction read and reread the pages of their books to find just the right way each page should sound. Sometimes they try it one way, scooping up the words, and sometimes they read it another way, using their voices to punch out some words."

During your teaching, show students parts of a text that you have already read with them. You could use your shared reading book, *Owls*. Ask students to listen to you read and reread part of the text aloud. You might say to your readers, "I am going to read this part with a lively voice. But I may encounter a challenge. If I do, I will try to reread this part, thinking about how to read it better. When you think I sound like the Kratt brothers, put your thumb on your knee. Then I will know which way sounds better."

As you demonstrate, you will want to voice over a few tips that show adjustments and changes you are making as you read and reread the page. Tell students that many readers reread the page to make it sound just right! Say things like, "I need to reread that and scoop up more words," or "I am going to say that key word stronger," or "Did you hear how I read that part with a lot of curiosity in my voice?"

Then, debrief what you did. You might say, "I saw a lot of thumbs on your knees when I had more emotion in my voice and when I reread parts a bit faster, scooping up more words and making some words sound stronger."

During the active engagement, select another portion of the same text, *Owls*, to have students read together. You could say, "Let's reread this part in *Owls*, by Mary R. Dunn. As you reread this page, try to make the words sound lively and interesting. But if you encounter challenges, see if you can reread it a couple of different ways to find out which one sounds best. I will be the judge. I will use my thumb to show you if I think you sound like the Kratt brothers!"

In your link, you'll want to rally your students around the important work they have to do. Say something like, "Now, as you go off to read, you have a whole bunch of things to do that will help you learn more about the world! As you learn more and more, working through the challenges in your books, aim to reread the pages like gold to find the just-right sound of each page. Sometimes, you might need to try it a couple of times, a couple of different ways."

Invite students to read quietly in the meeting area, using their best voices. Move around the carpet, listening to their reading. When you hear a child try to scoop up more words or reread a key word, emphasizing it, commend that reader publicly. You might say, "Sara, you reread that part like gold. You made it sound so lively! Off you go to your reading spot. Keep going." or "Wow, Carl, you tried that page three ways! I like how you kept trying to hear which one sounded best. That third time you read it was a charm! Off you go to your reading spot to keep reading." Highlight four or five students and then send the rest of your students off to their spots as well.

CONFERRING AND SMALL-GROUP WORK

As you circulate around the room to confer with small groups today, have some quick conferences that help you assess your students' level of fluency. Move from student to student, asking how many times they have read their books. Ask each child to tell you what his book is teaching and then listen to the child read. Think about what is important to compliment and teach. Consider the degree to which students are word solving on the run, reading words with automaticity, phrasing to preserve the syntax of the text, and reading with expression. Note whether students are rereading to make it sound smoother and to make sure that what they read makes sense.

You may also consider whether there is a small group of students that could use your support with any of the big teaching you have done in this bend, especially around key words. Or you might lead a small group of partners, coaching them to work together to find, chat about, and use key words that they find in their books.

Lastly, meet with any of the small groups you have worked with previously during the unit. Pull them together to check in about how well students are using any strategies you have reinforced during their small-group time with new books. In the early childhood classroom, repetition of teaching should be expected. Don't feel discouraged. Part of the developmental path of a young child involves forgetting and being reminded often of important things to do and try. Transfer is what you are after; therefore, try to coach students not only to use strategies they learn *one* way in *one* book, but to reuse strategies in *all* books.

Mid–Workshop Teaching

In your mid-workshop teaching, you might want to address another common problem readers at this stage have with fluency. By now, most of your readers will have moved past level D books, which means that they do not need to track word by word, yet some may continue to do so, using their fingers. Encourage students to practice tracking and scooping up more words with their eyes. Knowing *when* to use their fingers and when to pull them away is important for readers at this stage and has important repercussions for their level of fluency.

Address this by saying, "Readers, I see that some of you are using your fingers as you read. Now that you are stronger readers, fingers can actually *slow* you down. If you need to use your finger to do a slow check, take it out and put it under the word. If you *lose* your spot as you are reading, use your finger to help orient yourself. Make sure you are back on track, reading the words. *But then*, remember to take your finger *away* and use your eyes to scoop up the words and your voice to make the words sound important."

Transition to Partner Time

Partnerships can practice reading their books aloud, listening to how their voices sound and giving each other tips to read parts better. You might say, "Partners, be sure to listen to each other carefully, offering little tips so that you are both ready to read your book to another partnership. Listen to each other read and give each other a thumbs up when the reading sounds like the Kratt brothers! Give each other tips to make the reading even better. Say, 'Read it with more feeling!' or 'Reread that and scoop up more words,' or 'Make that word sound stronger.'

SHARE

Today's share session will be celebratory in nature. Have students get together with a different partner to share their books. Have the new partners read to each other in their best voices. Then give the new duo a chance to talk about questions and comments they have about each other's topics and books. Since readers will have prepared a couple of books, you might have them switch partners again, just as they did during the grown-up party earlier in the bend—or they could just stay with the same person. Either way, students can then share the next book they prepared to read.

At the end of the session, you may say to students, "Before we wrap up our session today, let's make a giant circle and read out loud our most important pages into the circle. Find a really important sentence or page, and rehearse it out loud or in your mind. Then, when I wave my pointer in your direction, read your part out loud, in your best reading voice."

Finding Interesting Things to Share

IN THIS SESSION, you'll teach children that to read books aloud well to others, readers first must figure out what they find interesting about the book. They must read the book and consider what about it is worth sharing with other people.

GETTING READY

✔ Prepare several pages of the first mentor text you used in this unit with Post-its marking places to talk about the text. We use pages 12–13 and 18–19 from *Hang On, Monkey!*, by Susan B. Neuman (see Connection, Teaching, and Active Engagement).

✔ Display the anchor chart "How to Get Super Smart about Nonfiction Topics" from Bend I so children can easily see it and refer to it (see Teaching and Active Engagement).

✔ Plan ahead to visit another classroom today so that your students can read aloud to other students (see Share).

✔ Display the anchor chart "How to Read Aloud Like an Expert" (see Share).

✔ Prepare the strategy Post-it—"Mark interesting parts (using the charts as a guide)."—to add to the chart (see Share).

MINILESSON

CONNECTION

Invite children to recall the things they have learned to do in this unit, applying that learning to a page of the first demonstration text.

"Readers, we only have another week or so in our unit of study on nonfiction reading, so I have been thinking and thinking about the most important work you all should do before this unit comes to an end. I went back and looked at the first book we read together. Remember this one?" I said, as I projected the first page of *Hang On, Monkey!* under the document camera.

"Do you remember the kinds of things we learned to do in this book? First, just think. When you've thought of a few things we learned to do, put your thumb on your knee." When many kids had their thumbs on their knees, I said, "Now, turn and tell your partner a few things we learned to do when we were using this book." I moved about the meeting area and listened in as kids shared. "We learned a lot of facts, like the monkey's tail helps it hang," Some kids began reading the text aloud to their partners, while others pointed to the anchor chart from the first bend.

Tell children that they are ready to teach this unit on their own, and invite them each to prepare a stack of books to teach to second-graders.

After they'd exhausted that one page, I said, "I knew it! I knew you could show so many of the things we learned earlier in this unit. Now this time, you can really do it all on your own. It's like I could go to another classroom," and I got out of my chair and walked toward the door, "and you could sit in my chair and teach this unit to . . . to who? Ms. MacDonald's class of second-graders? They, too, are studying nonfiction reading!"

Still standing away from my chair, I said, "You may think I'm joking about you guys taking my place in the teacher's chair, but I'm not. I'm thinking that you could each get together a collection of nonfiction books that you know really well, and you could go to another class and read those books with a kid in that class—*if* you are willing.

"To do that, you'd need to work on reading a small stack of books really, really well. Well enough to practically perform those books. After all, that is what I do whenever I am going to do a whole-class read-aloud with you. You game?"

❧ **Name the teaching point.**

"Today I want to teach you that to share a book like an expert, you first need to notice things that are worth sharing. It helps to mark pages where you found something interesting or important in some way—parts that made you sit up and think or wonder, to want to learn more."

TEACHING

Demonstrate what you did to prepare to teach the demonstration text to the class.

"The truth is, long, long ago, at the start of this unit, that is exactly what I did to get ready to read *Hang On, Monkey!* with you. First, I read it to myself, and I found parts that seemed important, parts I knew you'd find interesting, too. Then, I marked those parts to remember what to say out loud to you when I was talking about the book. Let me show you what I mean."

I projected pages 18 and 19 of the text, with an arrow pointing to the picture. "First, I stopped and studied this page. Next, I marked it with a Post-it. I drew an arrow to the picture so that when I read this part out loud I would remember to say all the things I noticed in the picture."

I pointed to the "Stop and study each page" bullet from the "How to Get Super Smart about Nonfiction Topics" chart from the first bend. "Let me show you how that looks. Watch me!" I held up the book to demonstrate.

"After I read the page out loud, I can tell my listeners all about the picture. I can say to my listeners, 'They eat bananas, flowers, and even insects.' Hmm, . . . I notice that monkeys eat with their hands and feet! Monkeys eat *lots* of things.' Finally, I want my listener to think, *too*, so I might ask, 'What do *you* see on this page?'"

Recap your process in a way that helps children replicate it.

"This is a great page to stop and think together. Do you see how first I found a part that was really interesting and then thought about what I would study on the page *with* my listener? Next, I marked it with the Post-it, to remind me to talk to my listeners after I read the words. That way, I can read these pages like an expert because there's so much to learn that's interesting."

FIG. 13–1   This student's plan for Read Aloud: "I want to ask, 'What does this family do together in their house?' Then I will say how I see the family eating together. And I will ask my partner, 'What do you see?' Then I will have her guess what she will learn next. And then I will say what I see and what is happening and have my partner do the same."

ACTIVE ENGAGEMENT

Remind students to use all the strategies they have learned for reading to themselves when they prepare to read to someone else.

"Let's remember all the things readers do to get super smart about nonfiction topics. Then, you can choose the parts you find *most* interesting and important and decide how to mark those parts to remind you what to talk about with someone *else*. Here's our chart! Let's quickly read it together."

ANCHOR CHART

How to Get Super Smart
about Nonfiction Topics

- Take a sneak peek to start learning.
- Stop and study each page.
- Guess what might come next.
- Chat about a page or the book.
- Make your voice sound smooth & lively.
- Find and think about key words.

Prompt partners to study another page to consider what they might say and wonder when reading aloud.

"Let's move to another part of *Hang On, Monkey!* that so many of us found to be interesting before. Read with me," I said, projecting pages 12 and 13 of the text:

There are small monkeys.

There are big monkeys.

"Now reread the pages with your partner and think about what you would want to talk about with someone or what kind of question you might ask. Look at our chart about getting super smart and pick something. When you know what you want to do, put your thumb on your knee so I know you are ready. Go ahead, tell your partner what you would do." I leaned in and listened while children talked for just a minute. Then I convened the class.

"I can tell that you really know this book, and that you would read it like an expert! Layla and Mark said that they would mark the page to chat about baby monkeys and the things that they are doing, like hanging on and hugging and staying close to the mama monkeys. Darren said that he would ask his listener, 'Guess what comes next?' to get the reader thinking about the information in the book."

There are small monkeys.

golden lion tamarins

80

I pointed to page 13. "Jordan and Zayd said that the big monkey—this one is called a mandrill—looks like a clown with its bright red nose. What *else* do you notice?" I nudged the other students to add on.

"I see purple hair on his butt!" Wilson chuckled, pointing to the photograph.

"You are noticing so much by stopping and studying the page. Did you see how I asked you, 'What *else* do you notice?' You can do that with your listeners as well! It helps them to see and say more.

"Do you see how marking the parts *you* find most interesting, will help *others* find them interesting as well? Think about *what* you want to say about those parts to help others learn more, see more, and say more about your topic!"

LINK

Send children off to reread books they've enjoyed, using ideas from the anchor chart to mark parts to share with an audience.

"We have a really nice plan for reading this book aloud and sharing it like an expert! We'll have to decide who we should read it to. Maybe the principal? Do you think she'd like it?" The children nodded in agreement.

"When you enjoy a book, you can mark the parts you want to share—the parts you hope other people will also find as interesting as you do. That way, when you read the book, you can think about what you want to say and what you want to ask others to say as you read. You can get ready to read the book like an expert.

"Now it's your turn! Pick the books you've read during this unit that you love most! Because if you are going to read a book aloud to someone else, it helps to really love that book. Get those ready to share and read like an expert!"

FIG. 13–2 This student's plan for Read Aloud:"I am going to ask a lot of questions. 'Why did Jessica's mom fix cars?' and 'How does Robby's dad cut hair?' and 'Why did Will's mom designs buildings?' Then I will say, "What does your mom or dad or grandma do?"

When asked if she had answers to these questions, she responded, "Yes! Of course! Like I think Jessica's mom is fixing the car because someone broke down and the car couldn't move. So, she has to fix it. It's her job."

Using Table Conferences to Support Fluency, Determining Importance, and Thinking about the Text

Circulate throughout the room, coaching individuals and conducting table conferences.

At the start of this final bend, channel students to return to concepts you taught in Bend I to practice and hone some essential skills. Supporting students in reading and preparing for reading aloud to others will not only help readers work on fluency, but it will also improve their comprehension.

Take a minute to look around your classroom and observe your readers. Do your students have Post-it notes and pens on their tables? Are students marking up parts of books? Are students rereading books?

You may decide to begin with a couple of table conferences based on your observations. You might say to a group of readers, "I see how you have your Post-it notes beside you, and how some of you have already finished a book, but oops, you forgot to mark parts you found really interesting. Do that now. Reread your books a couple of times and think, '*What* parts should I talk about, and then *how* will I talk about them?'" Move around the table, coaching kids to read and stop to plan. Direct them to the anchor chart if they are unsure what to say.

MID-WORKSHOP TEACHING
Asking Questions to Notice (and Say) More

"When you are preparing to read a book aloud, don't just pass by the little treasures that are hidden in the book! It helps to ask yourself, 'What is this teaching me?' or 'I bet this next page will teach me . . .' or 'What is happening here? What might come next?' Keep reading and rereading your books. Think about your plan, and don't forget the things you know about how to study pages and notice and say more!"

TRANSITION TO PARTNER TIME
Practicing Reading Aloud Like Experts

"Readers, it's time for your first read-aloud! I know you probably have a *few* books that you are ready to share. Partner 2, you can go first, and read aloud to Partner 1. Remember, your goal is to read your book like you're an expert! Get Partner 1 really hooked on your book. When you get to the places you marked, don't forget to stop and say what you notice and what you wonder. Then, get Partner 1 to think and talk with you. If Partner 1 has a hard time saying something, it's your job to help, just like a teacher would! Go ahead and begin your read-alouds!"

Share helpful suggestions and examples of successful planning with groups of students.

You also may decide to do a quick conference with one child and then coach the entire table of readers to emulate what that reader did. You might say, "Look at what Marcos did as a reader. He found four parts to talk about with his partner! He put a speech bubble on the parts where he is going to explain something and a question mark on the parts where he is going to ask his partner a question! Now he knows which parts to talk about and what to say. Look at the parts you marked. Are you ready for your reader? Reread your book and think, 'Will I say something about this part?' If so, make a speech bubble. Make a question mark if you are going to ask a question."

Listen to each member of the table, lightly scaffolding them to make decisions. Listen to exactly *what* they plan on asking and saying. If students are unsure, suggest that they choose a strategy from the chart or that they reread and then talk about what they are learning.

You may decide, intermittently, to voice over brief suggestions to the whole class. You might share reminders like, "Don't forget to mark more than one spot in your books!" or "Rereading will help you decide what you want to talk about with others." You might say, "Look at the question Marissa is going to ask," or "Ty just figured out what he is going to share with his listeners! Listen to what he is going to say." These little voiceovers, no more than a sentence or two long, help to engage and motivate readers. They also provide other children in the class with additional examples of what this work might look like and sound like. First-graders often rush through their reading, so they will benefit from the reminder to slow down and think as they read.

Reading Aloud to Another Class

Announce that the class will be reading their books to second-graders.

"Readers, are you ready to take a trip down the hall to visit another class?! Now that you've gotten some books ready to read, you can read them to *anyone*! And today, you're going to be sharing your books with the second-graders, who are *also* studying nonfiction! Each of you will get a special second-grade buddy to read to! So gather up your books and then quickly and quietly line up at the door."

Once you are in the second-grade classroom, explain to the second-graders how this read-aloud will work.

"Second-graders, your first-grade nonfiction reading buddy has prepared a read-aloud for you! You're going to hear some really wonderful books, and you'll hear your buddy's thinking about favorite parts, too. As your buddy reads, listen to the questions and thoughts your buddy has and add in your own thoughts, too! See if *together*, you *two* can grow a lot knowledge and become experts about an interesting topic!"

When you are back in your classroom, reiterate the importance of sharing books you read and topics you learn about with others.

"Readers, whenever you fall in love with a book or a topic, remember to share it! Spread your knowledge. You can chat about what you've learned, like you would chat at a pizza party, and you can also read the book—or favorite parts of it—aloud, like an expert, sharing all the things you notice. In the next week, we are going to continue to learn how to read books aloud and how to share them with an audience in powerful, beautiful, fun ways!"

I introduced the new anchor chart, "How to Read Aloud Like an Expert," and added the first strategy Post-it:

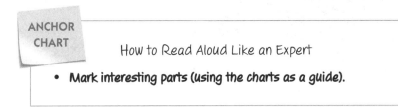

ANCHOR CHART

How to Read Aloud Like an Expert

• **Mark interesting parts (using the charts as a guide).**

Reading with Feeling

MINILESSON

CONNECTION

Tell children what a success their read-aloud to another class was yesterday, and invite them to discover other books to share with other audiences.

"The reading party we had yesterday with your second-grade nonfiction reading buddies was really fun! You taught your buddies *a lot*! Their teacher told me how excited they are now to learn even more about your topics. See how it pays off to mark parts and to practice reading a book like an expert when you want to share it with an audience? The second-graders loved hearing you read aloud so much that they decided to invite us back to their classroom, only this time, *they* are going to read aloud to *you*! Won't that be so much fun?!

"I'm sure you can imagine lots of other people you could read to next! You have book baggies filled with books, and we have a whole library with even more books waiting to be read and topics waiting to be discovered. Before we toss our books aside to say that we're done, let's really reread them and think about how we can read them like experts with our partners. What helps to make a read-aloud sound good?" Students offered some ideas.

❖ **Name the teaching point.**

"Today I want to teach you that to read a book like an expert, it helps to think about and practice *how* to read each part, making your voice show the feeling behind the words."

IN THIS SESSION, you'll teach children that when readers prepare to read a book aloud, they pay attention to how the different parts should sound so that their reading shows feeling.

GETTING READY

- ✔ Choose two parts of a shared reading text that children know well to read aloud in distinct voices. We use *Owls*, by Mary R. Dunn, the shared reading mentor text (see Teaching).

- ✔ Kids will need to bring a book from their book baggies to the meeting area, one that they have already read at least once (see Active Engagement and Share).

- ✔ Display the anchor chart "How to Read Aloud Like an Expert" so it is ready to refer to and extend (see Link, Mid-Workshop Teaching, and Transition to Partner Time).

- ✔ Prepare two strategy Post-its—"Show the feeling in each part." and "Figure out how the book is organized (Story or All About)."—to add to the chart (see Link and Mid-Workshop Teaching).

- ✔ Refer and reread parts of your shared reading text. We use *Owls* (see Share).

TEACHING

Model how to use the content of a page to figure out what kind of voice to use when you read it.

"Let me show you how I do this in *Owls*, by Mary R. Dunn. We know this book well! Remember the part about how owls get food?" I flipped to the page and held it up for children to see. "Oh, and how about the part that describes baby owls growing up?" I flipped to that page and showed it to the class. "Aww, they're so cute!" some kids called out.

"So let's see. If I want to read the part about how owls get food, I have to show how important it is that owls find something to eat, right? Because if they don't find food, they won't live! So let me put some urgency into my voice! Listen." I began to read the chapter "Finding Food" with a strong voice that conveyed seriousness and suspense:

Big eyes and keen ears help owls find their prey. They use sharp talons to grab mice, lizards, and birds.

I finished the section and then said, "What do you think? Did I show how urgent and important this information is? Now, when I read the chapter on how owls grow up, I'm going to keep in mind that the author is describing itty bitty baby owls. Listen to how I change my voice to show that." I began the chapter "Growing Up" using a softer, sweeter voice.

Female owls lay round, white eggs. Chicks hatch from the eggs in about 30 days. Male owls feed chicks many times each day. The young owls are strong enough to fly in five to seven weeks.

"Did you see how I read that part much more gently than the other part?" The children nodded.

Recap the work you did to consider the feeling of the words before reading them in voice that matched.

"Readers, for each part, I thought about the *feeling* that went with the section, and then I made my voice match to *show* the feeling. So when you reread your books, you will want to *first* remember what's happening in a part or on a page and *then* figure out how it should be read. Will you use a big, suspenseful voice," and I used my voice to show this, "a gentle, sweet voice," and I changed my voice again, "or some other kind of voice to show the feeling of the words?"

ACTIVE ENGAGEMENT

Channel partnerships to practice determining how parts of their own books should be read.

"Think you can try this with your partner now? Partner 1, take out a book you read yesterday. Start to read it to Partner 2. Think, 'What is this part saying? What kind of voice should I use to show the feeling in that part?' Partner 2, listen to see if you agree or to help your partner if he or she doesn't have an idea. Go ahead, read and think together, and

Starting the minilesson off with an inquiry can be a helpful way to launch a teaching point. It engages students and is an opportunity for you to assess what your students are able to articulate about the topic. An inquiry also generates a short list of criteria that you and your students can refer to throughout the workshop. You may decide to make this a one-day chart.

Regardless of the text they choose and the feeling that the pages evoke, support students to think flexibly, considering the different kinds of feelings they might show as they read aloud before deciding which matches the text best. You might also start helping kids recognize how long they should keep a particular feeling in their voices. Does it last one page or two? When does the feeling change?

Notice how students are asked not only to listen to, but also to evaluate and assess one another's reading. This helps raise the level of engagement.

then *reread* with your new voice. Then read it one more time. Make the first part of your book sound like an expert is reading it!"

LINK

Send children off to read the new books in their baggies like experts, marking interesting parts to share and changing their voices to match the feeling of each part.

"Ready to prepare the *new* books in your baggies to read aloud to an audience? That means you will have to know those books like experts. Will you read them just once? No way! You will read them a *few* times! Will you mark parts you want other people to notice? *Yes*, of course!

"Remember, your goal is to know your books so well that you can read them like an expert, with feeling, and be ready to share all the details you find most interesting. So you need to study your book, thinking, 'What feeling will I show with my voice for this part? For this next part?' Then make your voice match the feeling of each part. Today, this might mean that you don't read *all* the books in your baggie because you will be reading a few books *many* times!"

I added to the anchor chart that we started yesterday:

ANCHOR CHART

How to Read Aloud Like an Expert

- Mark interesting parts (using the charts as a guide).
- **Show the feeling in each part.**

Show the feeling in each part.

Arian reels and reels.
He pulls a shoe out of the river!

FIG. 14–1 Mathew marked this page, saying, "That's disgusting and surprising."

Wɦto Why Do you put egg on yourx

d thumbs

Paint the eggshell.
Make fun designs.

FIG. 14–2 After Carl wrote the Post-it he said, "I think because they don't want the egg to break and they have to be careful."

Supporting Students Who Are Reading at Higher Levels

Gather groups of students who are reading at higher levels to work with text features such as headings.

Today, plan to support readers both in increasing their fluency and expression, and also in thinking about their books and the information they are learning. Perhaps you might pull some of your higher-level readers together to support them in navigating some of their books.

Look at the types of texts and features that students are reading, and think about ways you can support them. You may find that with your higher-level readers, there are more text features, such as headings and subheadings, that they need to negotiate and use as readers. You might say to this group of readers, "As we read our books, many of the authors have given us *headings* to help us pay attention to what a section is mostly about. When we read a section, it's important to think about how the information fits together with the heading. If your book doesn't have headings, you might make one, to help make sure you know what the parts of your book are about. Let's read these two parts of *Big Babies and Little Babies* and do some of this work together. Then you can try it in your own books with a partner."

You may want to use a shared text first and then suggest that students use a book from their book baggies to work on this same skill with a partner. This will give students some practice at reapplication in their own just-right books. You might reconvene this group across a couple of days, leading students to work with more independence and flexibility in reading for and thinking about the main topic, not just of the whole book, but of each section.

Coach more fluent readers to remember to use basic word-solving skills when tackling more challenging words.

You might pull another group of higher-level readers who are still working on using different sources of information (meaning, structure, and visual sources) to solve words.

MID-WORKSHOP TEACHING
Noticing When the Parts of a Book Tell a Story

"Readers, as you study your books, figuring out how each part should sound, some of you are discovering that your books tell a story! For example, this book about race cars doesn't teach us about different *kinds* of race cars or even different *places* where drivers race. No, no, no! It teaches us what happens in one race, from the beginning of the race to the end! It tells us a *story* about a race. The parts of this book are the beginning, middle, and end. So to read it well, you would use your very best storytelling voice.

"Look at your books and think, 'Which information books tell stories?' and 'Which books have sections like "different kinds of" or "different parts of"?' You may also have books that give different types of information on *each* page, like *Hang On, Monkey!* Knowing how your book is organized will help you think about how to read it."

I added another strategy Post-it to the anchor chart:

ANCHOR CHART

How to Read Aloud Like an Expert

- Mark interesting parts (using the charts as a guide).
- Show the feeling in each part.
- **Figure out how the book is organized (Story or All About).**

Figure out how the book is organized.

TRANSITION TO PARTNER TIME   Reading Aloud with Feeling

"It's time to read with your partner! This is a perfect time to practice reading your books like experts, with feeling! Remember, one way to do that is to use voices that show the feeling of different parts. You can also stop at pages you've marked with a Post-it to say what you notice and wonder."

I gestured toward the "How to Read Aloud Like an Expert" chart to recap the strategies students had learned. "Use your time to practice reading your books out loud and talking about the details you've studied on each page. You might even listen to each other and think, 'What's another voice I might use to read that part?' Then, you can try out different ways to read the page and decide which voice sounds best."

For some students, especially if they are higher-level readers, they may be able to use their fluency to help them tackle harder print. Many of these students may not be used to encountering difficulty in their texts. See what students do in the face of a challenge. Coach students to use all they know to work on breaking down new longer and harder words. Then remind students to go back and reread to smooth out their reading and add feeling to show what this part of the text is trying to say.

Channel readers to think deeply about the text and its meaning to determine what feeling to show with their voices when reading aloud.

Some texts will demand that your higher-level readers read between the lines, making inferences and not just ingesting facts. To help readers think about the feeling of a part of the text, coach them to read and pause often to ask themselves, "Why is this information important?" or "What is the author trying to say here?" Then, after students think about those questions with you, you might say, "Now, let's look in the text and think about how you can show that with your voice."

Coach students to practice strategies and skills until they become internalized and automatic.

As you work with your readers one-on-one and in small groups, remember to coach students to work on implementing and practicing many of the strategies and skills you have been teaching with more efficiency and independence. Sometimes teachers are constantly thinking about what new thing they can teach a reader. Often the question should be, "How can I help the reader do this work more consistently, more independently, and in a more meaningful way?"

Practicing Reading Aloud Like Experts, Bringing Out Different Feelings

Invite students to read aloud in a circle. Challenge them to try out different ways to read their just-right books aloud.

I transitioned the class back to the meeting area, instructing the children to form a circle around the rug. Then, I began. "Readers, I asked you to bring one of your books to the meeting area because right now, you'll practice reading some parts aloud like an expert! I am going to call out a feeling, or a way to read a part in your book. Then, check your book and think, 'Is there a page in my book that I can read that way?' If so, you will read it out loud to us. Then we'll be able to hear and learn about different topics that are best read in similar ways.

"Ready? Here's the first way you can read: *strong*!" I didn't see anyone raise their hand or open their books. "Look through your book and think, 'Are there any parts I can read with a *strong* voice?'" I gave some time for children to reread, locating a page that compelled a strong voice. To support children's work, I demonstrated an example. "I have a part, remember?" I read the next part of "Finding Food" from *Owls* with a strong voice. Then I looked around to urge others to participate.

"I have a page!" one voice piped up.

"Read it into the circle with a *strong* voice!" I invited.

Afterward, I suggested another feeling. "Next, find a page to read with *excitement*!" A couple of kids read a page with excited voices. I continued with a couple more ways to read, to help students consider parts in their own books where their voices might show those feelings.

I commended the expressive voices readers were working to develop. "Wow, listen to this classroom! The sounds of your voices are absolutely precious. You are really thinking and rethinking the parts of your books to decide *how* they should sound. You are really sounding smart—like experts!"

FIG. 14–3 Shared reading of *Owls*.

Reading Like a Writer

MINILESSON

CONNECTION

Compare children to the authors of the nonfiction books they are reading.

"Yesterday, you really were thinking and rethinking just exactly *how* you should read the different parts and pages in your books. You noticed what the big feelings of different parts of your book were and then decided how to make your voice match those parts to sound like an expert!

"I realized something last night. Each one of you is just like the authors of the books we've been reading, because when you write, *you*, too, organize your information into chapters, don't you? Remember how in writing workshop we all studied this book?" I held up our mentor text from writing workshop. "Well, when you are getting ready to read the just-right books in your baggies aloud like experts, you can think and talk about them not only like *readers*, but also like *writers*."

❖ **Name the teaching point.**

"Today I want to teach you that to read a book like an expert, it helps to study all the parts you find interesting and important, thinking not just like a reader, but also like a writer. You might notice words that make a beautiful picture in your mind, or a part that makes you react in a big way or feel something."

IN THIS SESSION, you'll teach children that when they are planning a read-aloud, they can study what they admire about the author's writing. They can talk about those craft moves in their read-alouds, and they can also apply the same techniques to their own writing.

GETTING READY

✔ Bring a mentor text from writing workshop to show students. We use *Sharks!*, by Anne Scheiber (see Connection).

✔ Display a page from a demonstration text for reading, perhaps using a document camera. We use *Owls*, by Mary R. Dunn (see Teaching and Active Engagement and Conferring and Small-Group Work).

✔ Display the anchor chart "How Can I Teach My Readers?" from writing workshop. We use the chart from the first grade *Units of Study in Opinion, Information, and Narrative Writing: Nonfiction Chapter Books* (see Teaching and Active Engagement).

✔ Display the anchor chart "How to Read Aloud Like an Expert" so it is ready to refer to and extend (see Link).

✔ Prepare the strategy Post-it—"Study books like a writer."—to add to the expert chart (see Link).

✔ Prepare preselected texts (at everyone's just-right level) or ask kids to find a book in their book baggies without headings, and provide Post-its to mark off sections and write headings (see Conferring and Small-Group Work).

✔ Prepare to ask children to bring one book they studied like a writer, their writing folders, and a writing utensil to the meeting area at the end of today's workshop (see Share).

TEACHING AND ACTIVE ENGAGEMENT

Invite children to reread a part of the read-aloud text with you, noticing things the author does that they admire.

"Let's reread *Owls*, and *this* time, let's not only make our voices sound like experts. Let's also read, noticing what Mary Dunn does as a writer that we admire—things we could try, too!" I drew students' attention to our "How Can I Teach My Readers?" chart. "If you don't notice anything, you can check for some of these things you've noticed in *other* nonfiction books."

This is a wonderful opportunity to connect what your students are learning in writing to what they are learning in reading. You can use the same book you used in writing workshop to study craft, and study that book in reading. You will want kids to know that they can study all books as writers. If you need more support, you may refer to Grade 1 Units of Study in Opinion, Information, and Narrative Writing: Nonfiction Chapter Books (Calkins et al.).

How Can I Teach My Readers?

- Think about questions my readers might have.
- Include pictures (teaching words, lines and arrows, zooming in).
- Give an example.
- Use shape, size, and color words.

I projected a page from *Owls* and invited the children to read aloud with me:

Night Hunters

Most owls sleep all day. These nocturnal birds wing their way through the night sky.

about 200 kinds of owls live around the world. They make their homes in other birds' nests or holes in trees.

Turning back to the class, I nudged readers to study the author's craft. "What did Mary Dunn do as a writer that you can try, too? One thing I notice is that she used a number to show how many kinds there are. Could you use numbers in your writing, to teach more?" I paused. Students nodded.

"Now you try. Use our chart if you need help. When you have an idea, put your thumb on your knee." I gave the class a moment to formulate a few ideas. Once I saw students were ready, I prompted them to share. "Now, turn and talk to your partner." I moved in to listen, coaching children to consider the kind of information the author taught her audience, as well as *how* she taught it. I gathered up several responses to voice back.

Share students' thinking in a way that it is transferable to other books.

After a moment, I shared several ideas. "So, the author tells us things that owls do. If I am writing a book about basketball, could I also write what players do? Yes! And I heard someone say, 'The photograph also shows *how* the bird is "winging" through the air at night.' The photograph is giving *more* information about *how* owls do things. Could you do that with the topic that you are writing about?" Many children nodded. "As you read aloud, you could point out things, just like this. You could then talk about what the picture shows."

I continued, "Someone else said that Mary included a map to teach where owls live. Thumbs up if you think you could try that, too—include a map or a diagram showing where things are that go with your topics." Thumbs went up. "And lastly, someone noticed that Mary gives *examples*, like different kinds of homes owls find! Might you give examples about information you are teaching in your books? You bet! Might you talk about examples when you're reading aloud? You might. I'm going to mark page 6 because you noticed *a lot* on this page about what you could do as writers! *And* as experts reading aloud!"

Read aloud another part of the demonstration text and channel students to notice more craft moves.

"Let's keep reading like writers, admiring what Mary has done." I read on, as children joined in.

Up Close!

Owls come in all sizes. Some owls weigh up to 9 pounds (4 kilograms). Other owls weigh less than 1 pound (.45 kg). Owls have grey-white or brown-orange feathers. Soft wing feathers help owls fly silently.

"What do you notice that you could try as a writer? Turn and talk." Again, I moved from partnership to partnership, coaching students to study the way the author helped make a picture in the reader's mind.

"Some of you noticed that Mary tells about the sizes and colors of owls. Could you do that in your book that you are writing? What if you were writing a book about trucks? Could you write about the sizes and colors? Surely! What about when you're planning your read-aloud? You could talk about sizes and colors if they are mentioned in your book or shown in the pictures.

"Wow, you admired *so* many things that Mary R. Dunn did as a writer. You could definitely try these things when you write your *own* books. You can also use what you noticed the author did to give you ideas for what to talk about when you read your books aloud."

LINK

Remind children of the ways they know to read aloud well. Then send them off to reread their books as writers, noticing craft moves.

"You know lots of ways to make your read-aloud sound like gold!" I pointed to the last bullet on the chart and said, "And you can even do work that carries over to your writing!"

I drew students' attention to the anchor chart "How to Read Aloud Like an Expert" and added the new strategy Post-it.

ANCHOR CHART

How to Read Aloud Like an Expert

- Mark interesting parts (using the charts as a guide).
- Show the feeling in each part.
- Figure out how the book is organized (Story or All About).
- **Study books like a writer.**

Study books like a writer.

"When you go off to read today, as you stack your books, stack the *same* ones you read yesterday at the top. Practice rereading those first, noticing the things in them you admire as a writer—the things you can talk about in your read-aloud and try in your own writing. When you're done, choose books you *didn't* yet read. *First*, study them like a reader. *Then*, study them again, but as a writer. Off you go!"

Supporting Students in Studying Craft and Structure, Reading Like Writers

Support students in working with their own nonfiction writing to help them understand how nonfiction books sometimes provide headings to highlight main topics or ideas for each section.

This is a good time to follow up with the group of readers you pulled together yesterday. Working with this group of students, you taught them how to use and pay attention to the subtopic headings in their books. You also suggested that some of their books may still be written in parts, though the authors may not have given the reader a table of contents or section headings.

To start this group, you may ask students to pull out their writing first. Ask them to read one chapter to a buddy in the group, and have the buddy try to guess what heading the writer gave that chapter. Then have them both check to make sure that the heading helps the reader know what the section is mostly about.

Channel students to develop headings for nonfiction books that don't have them.

Next, you might provide a preselected text (at everyone's just-right book level) or ask kids to find a book in their book baggie that does not have headings to guide the

MID-WORKSHOP TEACHING
Noting *What* an Author Did and *Why* It's Helpful

"Look at one of the parts you admired and marked—a part where you noticed something special the author did. Turn to the person next to you. See if you can say *what* the author did and *why* you think it's helpful. Give it a try. Give your partner a chance, too. If you have a hard time, help each other. After each of you has practiced that once, keep on reading!"

TRANSITION TO PARTNER TIME
Considering an Author's Choices

"As you read aloud to your partner today, one thing you can do when you pause at a part you admire is notice the choice the author made to write what she did instead of saying it another way. You could say, 'Do you see here, that the writer *could have* said . . . but *instead*, she said . . .'

"You two could work *together* to decide why the writer might have made those choices! Make sure both of you get a chance to read each of your books aloud like writers. When you are done, go on to a different book, and look at it and talk about it, either as a reader *or* as a writer *or* both."

reader. Perhaps you will say to these readers, "Just as you make headings in your own books as you write, you can do the same as you read. This will help you make sure you are thinking about the various parts of the book and are able to remember what each part is mostly about."

Give students Post-its to mark off sections and to write headings that support the main topic or idea of each section. As you coach students, prompt them to show you the details that helped them form the title. Make sure you give students feedback on what they decide.

Coach readers to read like writers, not only noticing craft moves, but considering *why* the author might have made a particular move.

You might also check in with some of your higher-level readers to see what sorts of things they are noticing authors have done that they can try in their own writing. As you confer with some of these readers, you could ask them not only to show you what they noticed, but to begin to probe why the author might have made a specific choice. This question may stump some of your readers. You might model your own thinking, providing them with a few possible answers, to show them how to hypothesize and answer. You might say, for instance, as you display the page in *Owls* that you read earlier, "I like the way Mary Dunn uses the word *wing* instead of *fly* here, because it helps to paint a picture in my mind of the owl's big wings, open wide as it soars through the sky. I also like how she says 'night sky' to help explain what the key word *nocturnal* means."

Help your students practice this with other craft moves that they notice. Coach students to hypothesize different possibilities and then suggest, "So, in your own writing, when you want teach someone something new, you, too, can do what this author did, and . . ."

Support students who are having trouble identifying craft moves.

For students who are having a difficult time identifying craft moves in the books they are reading, you might suggest that they try to think about some of the things that are listed on the anchor chart "How Can I Teach My Readers?" For example, you might say to a reader or a small group, "As we read this next page, let's think, how does the author teach us a new word, like a key word, or new information. Let's read a little and stop and think about that." Then coach students to see if the writer used a comparison, for example, or chose to write a description.

In many of the books that students are reading, there will be different ways that the writer does these things. Have your anchor chart available for students to find and name things. Then say to them, "Let's keep reading through this book and the others to see if they do that in the *same* way or different ways! This will not only help you learn those key words and new information, but it will give you *lots* of ideas of things you can do in your own writing. It might also give you ideas for what to talk about when reading those books aloud."

Trying Things Authors Do in Your Own Writing

Invite children to practice applying craft moves they admire in the books they are reading to their own information writing.

"Readers, bring one book you studied like a writer, your writing folder, and a pencil over to the meeting area." As children did this, I gathered up our writing chart and the shared writing book from our bulletin board near the writing center. I brought these over to the easel.

"Readers, when you find things in reading workshop that you can use in writing workshop, it's important to give them a try. You can think, 'Let me try this in my writing, right now!' Open up your book to the page where you saw the author doing something you wanted to try in your own writing. Now take out your information writing book. Look for a place where you can do that *same* thing. Then go ahead and do it!"

As children worked, I circulated, coaching them, and then voiced over tips to the whole group intermittently. "Make sure you can *name* what the writer did. Use our chart if that helps," or "Try out what the author did in your writing!" or "Reread your writing and find a good place where you can add more and teach more." "Don't copy the author's *words*, but try to use the same *strategy*. For example, you might say to yourself, 'I'm going to try to use more words to describe what this looks like.' Go ahead now. What will you try?"

As students tried to apply techniques authors used to their own writing, I shared some examples of what they had done. "Listen to how Jermaine compared two things, explaining what was the same and what was different about them. . ." "Now hear how Sasha describes the sounds of the place she's talking about." Then I said, "Try this again! Find something else an author did, and then try that in your writing." After students had tried a few different craft moves, I had them reread those parts.

Then I wrapped up the session by saying, "When you read like a writer, not only can you notice *lots* of things a writer did to teach you more about a topic, but you can also learn things that *you* can try in your *own* writing! So make sure you always have your book baggies available in writing workshop, in case you need help from your authors!"

Readers Plan to Talk and Think about Key Words

MINILESSON

In the connection, remind students of all the ways that they have been planning and practicing reading their books aloud to one another. Tell students that they not only *sound* like teachers but actually *are* teachers; they are opening up new worlds to one another. You might share stories of partners you've observed. You could say something like, "Mariela got so excited about the topic of one of Sebastian's books—seahorses! They talked and talked and talked about all the pages in his book. You see, when your partner reads aloud to you, it can get you excited about the topic of that book! Here's the best part: soon, you'll *both* become experts about the topic."

You might go on to say, "Readers, when you're planning your read-aloud, thinking like readers *and* writers, make sure to point out and use those keywords you've already been collecting and thinking about, so that your audience can become experts, just like you! Sometimes *listeners* let the words just go right by them, and they need a teacher, or an experienced reader like you, to stop and remind them to think about those key words."

Then, name the teaching point. You might say, "Today I want to teach you that another way to make your read-aloud sound like an expert is to point out key words in your books as you read. You can use those words to talk about the topic, teaching others what they mean and why they're important."

In the teaching, you might start by reminding students of the key words you collected from your demonstration text, earlier in the unit. You might remind kids of that lesson, saying, "Remember how we learned that as you read you can jot down key words—words that are important to the topic of the book. Thumbs up if you've still been collecting key words as you read."

With the key words from the demonstration text in a pocket chart nearby, you might then demonstrate how, when you read aloud, you stop when you get to one of those words so that you can explain what it means and why it's important to the topic. "The person you're reading to really needs to know those important key words," you might say, "so you probably don't just want to read aloud straight through all of them!" Jot one of the key words from the demonstration text *Superstorm*, which you used during Read-Aloud, on a Post-it—*hailstones*, for example—and stick it to the page where it first appears, to show kids how the Post-it will be a reminder to stop and talk about the key word. You might then demonstrate how that explanation might sound, modeling a read-aloud of the page, stopping to define the key word and explain its relevance to the information on the page.

Then debrief, naming what you did as a reader. You might say, "Did you see how I found a key word, jotted it on a Post-it note, and planned how to explain what it means and why it's important?"

During the active engagement, you may want to invite students to try the same strategy in another book, such as your shared reading text. You might use the "Finding Food" chapter in *Owls*, reading a bit, then stopping for kids to practice choosing a keyword to spotlight. Ask students to turn and talk about which key word they want to mark. Share a few suggestions kids make, then choose one of the words to mark on a Post-it. You might say, "If *prey* is the key word you want your listeners to think about, what can you say to help them understand what it means and why it's important to the topic? Turn and talk about that with your partner."

During this turn-and-talk, coach kids to think about questions they can raise and answers they can give. Then debrief with your readers, saying something like, "Bravo, readers! You worked hard to make a plan for helping your listeners think about key words in your book."

Link today's lesson to students' ongoing work, reminding students to draw upon all they know to make their reading sound like experts, planning read-alouds that introduce listeners to new topics and teach them about the world. Recap today's teaching point, encouraging children to consider what key words in their books are particularly important. You might give students extra Post-it notes in their baggies to practice this work independently.

Add this strategy to your chart, and then quickly prompt kids to set a goal for using it. Ask readers to turn and talk about which book they will read first and what strategies they'll try. Share a few examples and send students off to read.

ANCHOR CHART

How to Read Aloud Like an Expert

- Mark interesting parts (using the charts as a guide).
- Show the feeling in each part.
- Figure out how the book is organized (Story or All About).
- Study books like a writer.
- **Explain and think about the key words.**

FIG. 16–1   Partners reading aloud together

CONFERRING AND SMALL-GROUP WORK

As you circulate around the room to confer and work with small groups today, reserve some time to check in with your higher-level readers. You may decide to pull them into a small group with their reading partners to scaffold their thinking about some of the key words or new vocabulary in their books. As your students become higher-level readers, the vocabulary they encounter will become more domain-specific, and the concepts they read about will be more sophisticated. For example, you may have students who are reading books about planets or gravity or other such topics that involve abstract concepts and include vocabulary that is harder to comprehend.

Also, higher-level readers may not be used to encountering difficulty and therefore may tend to speed through words they can pronounce but don't necessarily understand. In this small group, try to coach these readers to slow down and monitor for meaning, pausing at unfamiliar words and working to understand them.

You may say to these readers, "I took a peek at each of your books and placed four Post-it notes in each one. I thought you and your partner could first work in Partner 1's book and then switch to work in Partner 2's book. Two of the Post-it notes have a key word written on them. When you get to those pages, I want you to stop and work together to figure out what the word means. The next two Post-it notes are blank, and you'll have to figure out what key words to jot down *and* what they mean. Remember, slowing down and zooming in on key words will help you learn even *more* about your topics."

Coach partners to work together to problem solve the key words, using context clues and photographs to help define these. Once they have done this for one partner's book, prompt them to switch. "You did a great job with Partner 1's book. Now work with Partner 2's book. I'll check on you in about five to eight minutes. When you are done, keep practicing this on your own. Slow down and notice the key words, especially the new and harder-to-explain ones!"

This will allow you to check in with other students in the room. Research what readers have planned and practiced with their own books. You might investigate questions such as "Has the reader planned places to stop and notice and teach details?" or "Has the reader marked places to share questions?" and "Does the reader have some potential answers for those questions?" If the answer is no, you may want to coach children to add more to plan for their read-alouds. You might say, "One thing that teachers do when they plan a read-aloud is to make notes about lots of different kinds of talk. They say what they notice *and* what they wonder, *and* they even say answers to their questions. Let's practice that together."

Mid-Workshop Teaching

Address any problems that students might have making plans or deciding what to think and talk about. Stand in the center of the room and call out little voiceovers to help. For example, you may notice that many of your students only try one of the strategies on the chart, just one time. Remind them that they can use these strategies over and over with their books. You might say, "Readers, remember, you can guess what the next page is going to teach, not just once, but again and again throughout your books!"

Transition to Partner Time

As you transition to partner time, remind your readers to introduce the type of book they are reading aloud to their partners. Alert listening partners to listen closely to their reading partners, and also to seek help when they need it. You might say, "Listeners, if your partner says something or asks something that you don't understand, should you just sit there and *pretend* like you understand? No, no, no! Remember, readers ask for help! Say, 'I don't understand' or 'What do you mean?' or 'Can you give me an example?' This way your partner knows when he or she needs to explain more or say it another way!"

SHARE

You may want to invite your students to listen to each other plan and read their books aloud. Set your students up to hear three different read-alouds from their peers. They can listen and talk during the read-aloud. Then afterward, they can share and discuss *how* they planned their read-alouds and what they did that *any* reader could try. After the read-aloud, you might ask students, "Which of these things did you notice the reader do to read this book like an expert? Let's talk about it. Can you try those things, too, with your books? Yup, you can! Let's listen to the next read-aloud. Get ready to learn about the world! Get ready to hear this book read like an expert!"

Using Drama to Bring Your Read-Aloud to Life

IN THIS SESSION, you'll teach children that readers can use not only their voice, but also their body to bring a book to life.

GETTING READY

✓ Select a page or two from your demonstration text to model dramatization. We use *Owls*, by Mary R. Dunn (see Teaching).

✓ Prepare for children to bring their book baggies to the meeting area (see Active Engagement and Share).

✓ Display the anchor chart "How to Read Aloud Like an Expert" so it is ready to refer to and extend (see Link, Mid-Workshop Teaching, and Share). ✋

✓ Prepare the strategy Post-it—"Use drama to bring the topic to life!"—to add to the chart (see Link). ✋

✓ Display the anchor chart "How to Get Super Smart about Nonfiction Topics" (see Share). ✋

MINILESSON

CONNECTION

Make a connection to a familiar experience with dramatic play.

"Readers, you have been marking parts and reading your books aloud to your friends, and you have been showing them a *whole world* of new information. When you read aloud, you can help your listeners understand the topic, not only with your voice, but also with your body!

"You know how during choice time, we have our dramatic play center? You all have been really playing up the neighborhood jobs we have been learning about in social studies, and earlier this year, you brought to life many of the stories we read together as a class as well! You've been using that dramatic play center in *so* many different ways.

"Well, in reading nonfiction books, there are many things we can do with drama to help explain the information in our books, and to have *fun*!"

❖ **Name the teaching point.**

"Today I want to teach you that when you are reading aloud a book like an expert, it's helpful to bring the book to life, not just with your voice, but also with your body."

TEACHING

Model how you use your body to help convey information in a book with two parts of the demonstration text. Invite children to do this with you, and suggest a few ways it might look.

"During choice time, when you act out neighborhood jobs, I've seen you making little gestures, expressions with your face, and actions with your whole body. When I watch you pretending and dramatizing, I see you using your body. Using your body during reading means making gestures, actions, or expressions that help explain information in the book."

I picked up *Owls* and said, "As you're reading, and you come upon some important information in your book, you can read that part with feeling in your voice, and you can also show what that part looks like with your body. For example, here in our *Owls* book, it says):

> *Owls gulp small prey in one bite.*

"Go ahead. Right now, use your body to show, what does that really *look* like?" Kids started using their hands to pretend to eat.

"That's how *we* eat," I said. "*But* an owl doesn't have hands, and it swallows its food all in one bite, so I think it looks more like this." I dramatized tipping my head back, opening my jaws as wide as I could, and closing my mouth with a huge gulping motion to show how an owl's gulp might look. "Do you see how I'm trying to show you with my body what this part looks like, and that by doing this, I also show you what it means to gulp?"

The children nodded.

"Let's look at another part in *Owls*. I'll read it aloud, and I'll use my body to bring it to life. This time, you can do it with me!"

> *Female owls lay round, white eggs. Chicks hatch from the eggs in about 30 days.*

"What does that look like? Hatching?"

Kids started to push their arms toward the ceiling.

"Yes, I see what you mean. Maybe the baby owls—the chicks—use their wings to push through the eggshell, like this." I did the same with my arms, a bit bent, with an awkward movement. "But they don't look like they are that strong yet! So *maybe* the chicks use their beaks! *Maybe* it looks more like this." I started to make a pecking motion toward the ceiling with my nose raised, and lots of kids copied my gesture.

Primary readers learn so much through dramatic play. They build oral language skills, vocabulary, and social skills. Using drama in reading both engages your youngest readers in their work and sets them up to share their understandings with one another in developmentally appropriate ways.

Image of owl chicks FLPA/Alamy

Growing Up

Female owls lay round, white eggs. Chicks hatch from the eggs in about 30 days.

Debrief. Reiterate that drama can help readers and their audiences understand information.

"That was super fun! Acting a book out, using your body, helps you and your listeners really imagine and understand what's happening. Using your body can help you explain the information!"

ACTIVE ENGAGEMENT

Invite children to take turns with their partners, bringing books in their baggies to life using gestures. Offer coaching tips for each role.

"Okay, ready to try this with one of the books that you have already read on your own? Partner 2, will you go first and pick a book that you know well from your baggie? Reread the beginning of it with Partner 1, and find a part that is a good place to help explain and *show* what something important means using your body.

"When you find that part, stop and show your partner what you see. Use your body—your fingers, your arms, maybe even your face!

"Partner 2, don't forget to say to your partner, 'Is that what you see? Show me! Act out what you see!'"

Compliment children on a job well done.

"Wow, readers! Actually, I think I should call you actors. You brought your books to life just now! I could see you all using everything from your head," and I tapped my head, "to your toes," and I reached down to touch my toes, "to show what you see happening in your books. Bringing your book to life is fun, and it's also helpful in explaining the information in the book."

LINK

Remind children that, in addition to using their voices, they can use a little drama to bring a book to life. Remind them, too, of all that they now know about reading like experts.

"Remember, as you read on your own and with a partner, try to make what you're reading about come to life in your voice and in your mind! Sometimes, using a bit of drama—acting out a few parts—can help you explain what is happening.

"As you get ready to read your book and plan your read-aloud, you now know *so* many things that you can do to read aloud like an expert. Not only can you *sound* like an expert in your read-aloud, but you can also *look* and *feel* like an expert in your read-aloud!"

FIG. 17–1 Partners acting out how the snake puppet might move.

I added today's strategy Post-it to the anchor chart:

ANCHOR CHART

How to Read Aloud Like an Expert

- Mark interesting parts (using the charts as a guide).
- Show the feeling in each part.
- Figure out how the book is organized (Story or All About).
- Study books like a writer.
- Explain and think about the keywords.
- **Use drama to bring the topic to life!**

I explained to students that the next day they would have an opportunity to show off all they had learned in this unit, both about their topics and about reading nonfiction. I said, "Tomorrow, you'll have a chance to use all you know and all you've planned to read aloud like an expert at our nonfiction reading celebration!

"So, with that in mind, let's practice using drama as we read. Right now, I'm going to ask all the Partner 2s to set up for reading workshop and get started. Partner 1s, just start your reading here in the meeting area. I want you to have a chance to practice as well. As soon as I've seen you practice a bit in your book, then I will ask you, too, to go off to your reading spot."

Preparing for the Celebration by Rehearsing Read-Alouds

Coach students on fluency, expression, and drama as you circulate around the room and gather small groups for targeted support.

Today as you circle the room, conferring and pulling students into small groups, remember that you are both preparing students for their read-alouds tomorrow and also still coaching them as readers to improve their understanding as they read.

You may find that you have some overly enthusiastic dramatic readers who are trying to act out everything on the page. Stop these readers and pull them together. You might say to them, "Readers, remember, we don't want to just act out every page. We want to use our acting to explain information in our books. So, reread your book and

think about a couple of parts you can really bring to life. Then you can go back and decide *how* you will act it out to show what it means."

Coach students on their plans for stopping and talking about their books as they read aloud.

As they prepare for their read-alouds, students should be planning for a few different ways of stopping and talking about their books. If kids have exhausted their book baggies, they can always go into the library and select more books to read. Give students some feedback on the choices they are making about what to think and talk about with their visitors tomorrow. Ask them about their plans, and give them a compliment about which parts seem to work well. Then give them a quick tip, a piece of critical feedback, about how they can improve their plans. Remind them that what they try with this one book, they can do with all the books in their baggies.

MID-WORKSHOP TEACHING
Rereading Can Help Readers Do Their Best Work

"Readers, I just want to stop you, briefly. Some of you are *only* acting out parts and pages and aren't rereading your books. Remember, to become expert, you need to reread and think more! You could reread your book and try to guess what the next page is going to teach you—on every page. You could reread your book and stop and study every page!

"The chart is here to help you!" I said as I pointed to the "How to Read Like an Expert" chart.

"Make sure you have prepared read-aloud plans for all the books in your book baggies. Before marking the parts in your book to talk about during your read-aloud, you can always reread the book a few times, getting ready to read it like an expert. *Then*, go back and mark the *best* places to do your *best* thinking and talking!"

TRANSITION TO PARTNER TIME   Making Sure to Say Something When You Don't Understand Your Partner

"It's time to work with your partners and practice reading your books aloud! Partner 1, why don't you start today. As you listen, Partner 2, really think about what Partner 1 is showing you and helping you think about. Remember, if you are picturing something different, *say so*! If you are not understanding something, *say so*! And if you need your partner to reread a part . . ."

"Say so!" the children chimed in.

"Sometimes there is more than one way to understand and explain things. Sometimes we have different opinions, and sometimes we just make mistakes! Be the kind of partners who are on alert to help and to make sure that you both understand what's going on!"

Revising Your Read-Aloud Plans

Coach students to try out and revise their read-aloud plans, giving each other feedback in partnerships.

"Readers, tomorrow is your reading celebration. Guess who I invited *this* time to your reading celebration? I invited the *kindergarten* class from down the hall! They are going to come to our classroom to hear our read-alouds! They are going to learn *so* much about the world from you, the experts!" I flexed my muscles and pointed to our anchor chart about reading aloud like experts.

"Now, to prepare for your reading celebration, I think you should do the things that you do to get ready for your writing celebrations! Make sure that your read-aloud plans are as strong as possible so that your read-alouds really sound, look, and feel like an *expert*.

"As you work on your plans, consider, 'What should I change, add, or take out completely?' Then, *revise* your read-aloud plans." I motioned for one of the students to come up and sit in my chair.

"Karina has a plan for her read-aloud, and she wants feedback from you all. She wants to know what she should *revise* in her read-aloud plan. What should she change, add, or take out?" I pointed again to our anchor chart.

"Karina, you read aloud to us, and then *we* will discuss, as a class, what we think you should revise in your plan. Class, use this chart, 'How to Read Aloud Like an Expert,' and this chart, 'How to Get Super Smart about Nonfiction Topics,'" I said, bringing out the chart from our first bend, "to help you decide what you think her read-aloud needs. Go ahead, Karina, we're ready." I sat on the rug next to Karina's partner, ready to listen like one of the students in the class.

After she read to us, students suggested things like, "Karina should act out . . ." and "Maybe she could talk about the key word . . ." and "She should ask *us* some questions."

"These are great suggestions. Karina, do you want to make some of those changes to your read-aloud plan right now? I bet you do. That was so helpful, right Karina? Your advice really can help your classmates get ready for our celebration tomorrow. Will you and your partner each choose a book to get help with on trying out and revising your read-aloud plan? Remember, consider what your partner should change, add, or take out to really make his or her read-aloud sound, look, and feel like an expert."

A Celebration of Reading to Learn about the World

IN THIS SESSION, you'll teach children that when readers share a book with an audience like they are experts, they make sure that their audience is attentive and understands the information.

GETTING READY

✔ Prior to this session, invite a class of kindergartners to spend today's workshop with your class. Their teacher should explain that they will each get a reading buddy who will share some books with them.

✔ Mark a part of your demonstration text with Post-it notes to plan where to stop and talk. We use *Owls*, by Mary R. Dunn (see Teaching).

✔ Prepare to ask your students to bring their stacks of books with them to the meeting area (see Active Engagement and Link).

✔ Display the anchor chart "How to Read Aloud Like an Expert" for easy reference (see Link).

✔ Bring empty baskets and index cards to make new categories for books in the library (see Share).

MINILESSON

CONNECTION

Welcome the class of kindergartners attending your students' read-aloud celebration. Introduce your students as experts on various topics, and explain how the read-aloud will go. Then turn the reins over to your kids.

"Good morning, kindergartners! Welcome to our classroom! You have entered into a room full of experts who know *so much* about the world we live in. Each of these first-graders has been studying a topic and would like to share all that they know and think about it with you! They want to teach *you* about cool things like trucks, koala bears, and storms!

"The first-graders are going to be your teachers. They will read their books aloud to you. *You* can choose one of the books in their stacks, and they will read and talk with you about that book! When you are done, you can then choose a *new* book from their stack for them to read to you!

"Now, first-graders, you are in charge! You will be reading and helping your newest reading buddies listen and think with you!"

❖ **Name the teaching point.**

"Today I want to teach you that as you read your books aloud like experts, it's important to check in with your audience—your reading buddy—to make sure that he or she is *with* you, understanding the information you are sharing."

TEACHING

Demonstrate what it looks like to read aloud like an expert, making sure that your audience is with you—both paying attention and understanding the information you're sharing.

"We have lots of parts of *Owls* marked up and ready to read aloud to our new friends here today. Here's what we'll do. I'll quickly take the role of teacher, and first-graders and kindergartners, will you take the role of listeners? Will you be my audience? Let's show our kindergarten friends what it looks like to share a book like experts." I paused for effect. "Ready, everyone?"

They all nodded.

"I want you all to watch not only how I make my voice sound like an expert, but also how I am watching *you* to make sure that you are with me. Watch what I do and say!"

Voice over as you read aloud, pointing out the things you are doing to hold your audience's attention and to check that they understand the information you are sharing.

I started to read from *Owls*. Before I even said anything about the book, I pointed to the picture. "Are you looking here?" I looked at the group and then I looked back at the page. Then I said, "See, I am pointing to the picture to make sure I have your full attention!

"You might notice that I have Post-it notes all over my book. That's my plan for my read-aloud! Watch how I use the Post-its to help me remember where to stop and what to talk about." I kept reading. I dramatized the text using gestures. I used my voice to show feeling. Then I asked a question and explained a key word. I said, "Did you see that I didn't forget the plan on my Post-it notes? I said what I was thinking and wondering. Then I asked you to do the same. Okay, keep watching!" I kept reading and then interjected, "Did you understand that? Do you want me to read that again?"

"Yes, read it again!" the group shouted.

"See how I checked in? When you are reading with your new reading buddy from kindergarten, you too will want to check in with your buddy! You can point to pictures to help your buddy see what you are talking about, you can ask if they understand or want you to reread, and you can use your Post-it notes to remind you to talk with them about the pages and parts you marked."

By bringing in a younger group of kids, you set your first graders up to feel more like mentors or teachers than like little kids. Make sure everyone understands their roles and gets to practice being both listener and speaker. This will give the new partnerships a chance to practice the work together, before they are asked to go off and work independently.

ACTIVE ENGAGEMENT

Invite your students to read aloud to their kindergarten buddies, first practicing on the rug before going off to their individual reading spots. Coach children as they do this.

"Okay, right now with your buddy, let's have a quick practice before you go off to your reading spots. Ask your buddy to pick a book from your stack that he or she wants to hear and learn about. Then start your read-aloud. Check in and make sure your buddy is with you."

I then coached a few partnerships, every now and again voicing over to the whole group. I said things like, "Point to the picture and see if your buddy is looking at your book," or "Ask your buddy if she understands or wants you to reread," or "Don't forget your Post-it notes! Think and wonder with your buddy!"

LINK

Send your students off to read aloud to their kindergarten buddies, reminding them to let their buddies select the books they want to hear. Remind the two groups of their roles.

I reminded my first-graders that if they were to get stuck and weren't sure what to do, they could always rely on our anchor chart.

ANCHOR CHART

How to Read Aloud Like an Expert

- Mark interesting parts (using the charts as a guide).
- Show the feeling in each part.
- Figure out how the book is organized (Story or All About).
- Study books like a writer.
- Explain and think about the key words.
- Use drama to bring the topic to life!

"Now, readers and experts about the world, it's time to go off to your reading spots and read aloud! Remember, you have a stack of books. Read as many as you can. Let your buddy choose which one he or she wants to read first! Have fun and learn a *bunch*! Don't forget, check in with your buddy every now and again to make sure that he or she is with you, understanding what you're reading. Go ahead, experts, start your read-alouds! And kindergartners, be the very best listeners you can be, and above all, enjoy!"

Using Compliments to Celebrate and Reinforce New Strategies

ON THIS DAY, the day of the celebration, build your first-graders up with confidence. You can do this by giving them specific compliments that name the things that are going well and teach them what to keep doing. You may say something like, "I see how you are explaining to your buddy what is happening there. Pointing to pictures is really helpful." Or you might say, "Wow, your voice is really showing me and your buddy how dangerous that part is. Keep using your voice to show us the feeling in the book." Pointing out what students are doing well and why it's useful can help students remember and replicate specific reading strategies in the future.

Model listening and responding to read-alouds.

You may also decide to join a few partnerships as another "perfect partner." You may join the read-aloud, listening and responding, side by side with the kindergartner listeners. You may only stay for a couple of minutes. You might chime in with some of your own thinking to help engage both readers a bit more in their reading. You might say, "Really? I had no idea. Why does that happen?" Or, "Oh, yeah, I know an example of that! It's like . . ." Avoid overtaking the conversation, but model being responsive to the reading and showing genuine interest in the information.

Coach readers and listeners who might need extra support.

There may be some partnerships that need a little extra boost. Maybe it's hard for the first-grader to sound engaging, or it's hard to retain the kindergartner's attention. You might intervene with extra support. You might whisper to the kindergartner to help her engage more in the reading that the first-grader is doing. You might whisper, "Oh, did you know that?" or "What do you think of that?" or "Do you see that? Look closer at the page." Or you might whisper to the first-grade reader, saying things like, "Show him the picture. Make sure he is looking at the page." Or "Ask her a question. See what she thinks." Or "Show that to him so he can understand it better."

MID-WORKSHOP TEACHING
Doing *Something* When You Finish A Book

Compliment children on their read-alouds and remind them that when readers finish a book, they do something, such as work with their buddies to list the things that the book taught them.

"Kindergartners and first-graders, all nonfiction readers, can I have your eyes and minds here in the middle of the room?" I waited until I had their attention.

"I'm *so* impressed with your reading. It is really sounding golden. *And* I am very impressed with your talking—also golden. But remember, when you finish a book, do *something*! Don't forget to name across your fingers all the things that the book taught you. Do this with your kindergarten buddies first. Hear *all* the things that *they* remember first, and then you can help add on to that. Try this now and see what mini experts your buddies are becoming. Then keep reading."

Making New Book Baskets for the Classroom Library

Channel students to consider how to organize their nonfiction books.

"Readers, it's time to come together for our final share session in this unit. You and your new reading buddy just read a bunch of books about interesting things in the world. While the kindergartners are still here, this is the perfect time to think about how to arrange our library and make it super easy to find the books we *most* want to read. Since you have changed and grown so much as readers, so, too, can our library. We want it to be easy to find books on topics that we most want to read about to help us get even smarter about the world.

"So, buddies, look through your stack of books, and think about what type of basket would be best to put your book in so anyone can find it and study it. Turn and decide with your buddy what kind of baskets we should make."

Help students shift books from baggies to baskets labeled by topic.

After students had a chance to talk with their buddies, I said, "Okay, so, there are many ideas out there. We have suggestions for baskets called 'Things that fly,' 'All things under the water,' and 'Amazing places.' These are cool basket names! Look at your books with your buddies. Do any of you have books that fit into *these* categories? Reread your books to make sure they belong. Then hand your book to your buddy to come place it in the appropriate basket.

"I know there are more baskets that we should name. Let's get to it. Other suggestions?" We continued to name new baskets until we had a variety of baskets in the library with a selection of new books at varying levels in each. Because all of our baggies were now empty, I said to our readers, "Look at our new lovely library. We have so many cool books and interesting topics to read about! All your baggies are empty! You are going to need new books for the weekend and to read on Monday."

Invite students to choose new books for their baggies by topic from the new baskets.

"*Now* as you choose books, you can first think, 'What am I interested in studying? Things in the ocean?' Then you can go to the ocean basket and look for a just-right book in there that seems interesting. We are going to spend the last few minutes of workshop filling our baggies back up with just-right books that we want to read! Now as you shop, use our new topic baskets to help you find the best books to read!"

FIG. 18–1   New topic ideas for baskets in the library

Read-Aloud

Getting Ready: BOOK SELECTION

During the read-aloud time in this second unit, your aim will be to support students' growing understanding of how to think and talk about information from nonfiction books. You'll support students in understanding and being able to talk well about the information that they learn.

Select a book about an engaging topic that is a complex text above your students' just-right book level. You may choose a topic that complements your social studies or science curriculum or any topic of high interest to young readers. We selected *Super Storms*, by Seymour Simon, because it is a well-written, highly engaging nonfiction book. It is organized by different types of super storms, and it is the kind of book that grips students' attention through its descriptions of the storms, the damage they cause, and preventive measures people can take when faced with one of these dramatic natural phenomena. Weather is also a science topic that many first-graders study.

You might do this read-aloud toward the beginning of the unit and then use these lessons as models to plan read-alouds using different texts later in the unit to support and extend the work.

GETTING READY

✔ Choose a read-aloud book that is highly engaging and just above the independent reading level of most of your students. We selected *Super Storms*, by Seymour Simon.

✔ Insert yellow Post-its for the corresponding day into your copy of *Super Storms* to plan prompts to think aloud and tell students when to turn and talk.

✔ Create or display an accountable talk chart, such as "Readers TALK about Books" from the Read-Aloud in Unit 1: *Building Good Reading Habits*. 👆

✔ Display the chart from the current unit of study, "How to Get Super Smart about Nonfiction Topics."

Super Storms by Seymour Simon.

In this unit of study, you'll immerse your students in the genre of nonfiction reading, and you'll introduce them to many different topics along the way. Through this read-aloud experience, you'll support students' work on thinking, speaking, and listening skills to help them understand the nonfiction texts that you read. Not only will practicing these skills together help students understand the texts you read aloud, but it will help them internalize and apply the same skills when they read independently and with partners.

Just as in the rest of this unit of study, you'll help students set themselves up as readers and learn information from the book right from the start. You'll help them learn how to study a page and think about the main topics that books are teaching. You'll help students think about how texts are organized and make reasonable predictions about other information they will learn through reading.

A book like *Super Storms* may take a couple of days to read (twenty minutes each day), with turn-and-talks and think-alouds interspersed throughout the read-aloud. You may decide at the end of Day Two to have a whole-class discussion on the important information that Seymour Simon is teaching through his book. On Day Three, you may decide to revisit parts of the text and reread those parts to discuss them in more depth. In so doing, you'll provide a model for what you want students to do when they finish reading books as well.

The following read-aloud lessons are designed to be flexible and not necessarily dependent upon particular teaching from the unit. In other words, it is not necessary to wait until after a certain session in the unit to begin. Of course, the read-aloud does build upon and support work from the unit, so the more you reference teaching from the unit in your read-aloud and vice-versa, the more likely students will apply and transfer their learning.

FIG. 19–1 Students turn and talk during read-aloud.

BEFORE YOU READ

Introduce the book and take a sneak peek to preview the content.

Introduce students to the new read-aloud book. Before you do so, you also might want to introduce a key word from the text. Choose a word that is used frequently and is core to understanding the text. You might start off your introduction by saying, "Readers, I picked out a great topic and read-aloud book for us to study together and become super smart about. I chose the topic of storms and this book, *Super Storms*, by Seymour Simon. Some of you may already know quite a bit about super storms. Is that true? Well, I am curious. What is the difference between any old storm and a *super* storm? I hope this book will teach us that.

"Do you all know this word, *destruction*? Do you know what it means? Turn and tell your partner what you think it means. Try to give examples to show what it means." Write the word on a note card or on the easel, and then write words and phrases that students may use to explain the word, such as *damage*, *hurt*, *breaking things*. Then you might say something like, "I wonder what that has to do with super storms. If you have some ideas, keep them in your mind as we do our sneak peek. Ready?"

Then start your sneak peek. Begin by reading the title, then study the cover, and then read the back cover. You may decide to have students talk about what they are learning so far. You can prompt students to turn and talk by saying, "So, what are you already learning about super storms? Turn and talk. And don't forget to use this word." Point to the word that you already introduced.

Prompt students to monitor for meaning as they read. Then have them connect that information with the title of the book or the main topic of the page. You may decide to do a think-aloud after the preview that helps to build understanding of what you are learning now and what you expect the text to teach. For example, you could say, "I agree with many of you. Super storms are dangerous because they cause destruction, like tornados breaking homes and cars. They can cause lots of damage. I bet Seymour Simon will teach us about different types of super storms and the kind of damage and destruction they might cause. Who agrees?"

AS YOU READ

Invite students to think about and discuss the text to understand its meaning.

We have found that pacing and flow work well for this book when the first half of the text is read on the first day, and the text is finished on the second day. On the first day, as you begin you may want to ask students to turn and talk about examples of types of storms that they know and how they might be sudden

During a thunderstorm, lightning bolts can shoot between clouds and the ground. A bolt of lightning is 50,000 degrees. That's five times hotter than the surface of the sun. Lightning can destroy a tree or a small house. It can also start fires in forests and grasslands.

and violent, making sure they know what those words mean. You could prompt students to add details to their explanations by saying, "What examples are you thinking of? Remember to tell your partner *and* say why it is a super storm!"

Read the next couple of pages. Coach students to think about meaning and monitor for comprehension. There may not be any new words, but there will be a lot of information for students to absorb and understand, including numbers and ideas. What's most important is that students are practicing thinking about what the information means.

You might say on pages 6–7, "Wait, what does this mean: lightning can start fires in forests and grasslands? How does that relate to what Seymour Simon is teaching us about super storms?" This two-part question first gets students to think about what the information means and then helps them see how to fit it together with other information in the book. You may first do a think-aloud, answering the question. Then read the next few pages, ask the same questions, and have students turn and talk to answer them.

Then you might start the next part, carefully studying the picture of a street covered with hailstones on pages 10–11. Display it to the class and ask students, "What do we see? What is happening?" You might work on developing some new vocabulary words. First, assess your class to see if anyone knows a tricky word or how the word fits with the topic of the book. Then, get your readers to use the picture and the words to begin to describe this new word. Perhaps you will read the first word on the page, "Hailstones," and say to your class, "Does anyone know what kind of storm has hailstones?" Some students might. Say to your students, "Let's listen and discover *what* hailstones are." After you read the page, focus on the "zoom in" box and say, "So, what is a hailstorm? Explain it with your partner. Use the words and the picture to help you."

As you get ready to read the pages about the thunderstorms that hit New York State, you might start by reviewing some of the information that you have learned about super storms so far. Then, before you read the next section, you may want to give your students a listening prompt such as "As we read this part, let's keep thinking about how thunderstorms are dangerous and cause destruction. Let's think about some examples of this." After you read the section, you will want your readers to work on putting together the parts of what they just heard. Say to your students, "Now, let's turn and talk about what is important to know about thunderstorms. What are some examples of the destruction they might cause?" As you listen to your students, show the text so they can see the picture and the words. Some kids might talk about the trees that are snapped. Others might talk about animals losing homes in the trees.

Listen in while your students talk so that you can share with the whole class a couple of examples of what some said. Then, ask students to think about what they may learn next in the text. You might channel them to do this by saying, "So we've learned about thunderstorms and hailstorms. What do you think we will learn next? What will the next section be about? Turn and talk." Again, choose a few examples to share with the class. "Some of you said tornados, and others said maybe hurricanes or a snowstorm. Let's find out." Then, display pages 14 and 15 and read the pages on tornadoes.

As you read aloud about tornados, you might also think aloud, commenting on or chatting about what you are reading. "Can you see what is happening? I see the wind spinning and cars and houses in a funnel breaking apart! Whoa! I have so many things that I am thinking about here. You, too? If I were to chat about this part, I might say, 'Whoa, tornados

SESSION 1: AS YOU READ
pp. 10-11: Pause to share thinking.
"Let's study this picture. Think and talk about it. What do you see? What is happening?"
"Let's read this page to discover more about _____."
"Now, we just learned a lot of information about _____. Explain to your partner what this page just taught us."

are so fast and cause so much damage and destruction. And they are so dangerous to people!' Are you chatting with yourself? Keep thinking as I read this next part."

When you get to the map on pages 18 and 19, you might spend some time talking about it and showing students how to navigate both the map and the key. Then help them to discuss the information on these pages. You might say to your students, "Let's read this map together. Let's use the key to help us learn some important information about tornados. Like, what do these red spots mean?" You can also invite students to propose questions about this part of the text. Then, wrap up the conversation.

AFTER YOU READ

Review what students have learned so far and ask them to predict what's ahead.

You may want to stop here and read the rest of the book at the next session. As you bring the read-aloud to a close, solidify students' learning and help them to practice the important skill of retelling by reviewing all that they learned about super storms thus far. You could prompt students to think about what the book taught them so far by saying, "With your partner, see if you can tell all the things that the author, Seymour Simon, already taught about super storms. Use as many fingers as you can to remember and name as much as you can from the first part of the book." Then, as you listen to partners talk, prompt students to say a bit more with questions such as "What else did he teach us?" or "What is an example of that?" or "Why is that important to know?"

Then bring your students back together and say, "Okay, let's share what we've learned as a class. What's important to know about super storms?" After your students share, you might say, "What do we expect the next part of this book will teach us about super storms? Any ideas?" You may ask a few students to share their predictions and then say, "We will find out more tomorrow!"

SESSION 2

BEFORE YOU READ

Remind students to use what they know to help them understand new text.

As you start off your read-aloud work in this session, review what students remember from the previous session. Remind students to use what they already know to help them understand the new information they will learn about next. You might start by prompting students to retell the important things they learned from the first part of the book. Say to your students, "Yesterday we learned a lot about how super storms are . . ." Flip to the back cover and read it once again:

Storms are sudden, violent changes in the weather.

"What does that mean again? Partners, take turns sharing one example with each other." Share a few examples you overhear, and then turn to the pages that students talk about and say, "Many of you think that the next super storms we will learn about might be snowstorms, hurricanes, and maybe sandstorms. Let's take a sneak peek at the pictures to see if you were right and to learn more about super storms."

FIG. 19–2   Read aloud whole-class conversation

AS YOU READ

Channel students to engage with the text by asking and discussing questions about it.

As you read the pages about hurricanes, stop and study each page. You may want to ask students to help you answer questions about the text, such as "What does that mean?" or "What do you see happening?" You may pause after page 25 and ask students to raise their own questions about hurricanes. Invite students to turn and talk about their questions, and then ask for three or four examples to be shared with the whole group. Reread the text to see if it can help to answer the questions. Then read on, thinking about answers for the questions that remain open.

At the end of page 25, you might lead students to think about the main topic. Say to them, "So this part here, what was it mostly about? Turn and talk." To encourage them to give more detailed responses, you might say, "Try to say more than just what sort of storm it was." Then as you bring students back together, you could crystallize their responses by saying, "So, some of you think this part was about hurricanes and why they are so dangerous. If you agree, give a thumbs up. I do, too! Let's keep reading."

Before you read the pages on blizzards, encourage students to bring forward all they have learned thus far by asking them to think about what they know already about super storms. They will most likely list the types of storms they have learned about. You may remind students to think about what makes these storms super. If students have a hard time answering, remind them by saying, "We know that super storms move quickly and have strong winds. We know that they cause destruction and damage. We are about to read about blizzards. How do you think blizzards might be similar to tornados, thunderstorms, and hurricanes? Turn and talk!"

When you reach the last page, demonstrate for students the kind of work you do when you reach the end of a book by using thinking prompts to grow ideas about the text. You might pause after the first sentence and use the thinking prompt, "This means that . . ." You might say, "Seymour Simon teaches us here that 'No one can prevent storms.' That means there isn't anything I can do to make it *not* rain or to *stop* the lightening or to make a tornado *go away*. I have *no* control, and you have *no* control as well. People and animals can't *stop* super storms from happening."

After the second sentence, use the prompt "One example is . . . Another example is . . ." by saying, "One example of how weather reports can help us is they can tell us that a storm, which might cause a flood, is on the way—like a hurricane. Then people can prepare or evacuate or put things up on their houses to protect them from getting destroyed. Another example is if there is a tornado coming, when you hear the report, you can take cover in a basement or a shelter underground. After the last sentence, you might ask, "What does Seymour Simon mean by, 'The more prepared we are the safer we will be'? Turn and talk." As students talk, circulate among them, and coach them to extend their conversations by prompting them to give examples. You might say, for instance, "One example of that might be . . ." You might also invite students to add onto each other's ideas.

AFTER YOU READ

Engage students in a whole-class discussion about the book.

At the end of the read-aloud, leading your students in a whole-class conversation will provide an opportunity for them to discuss their thinking about the book and to further solidify the reading skills they are learning. To make the discussion as authentic and rich as possible, let students discuss the entire book and what they now know about super storms. Start by reminding students about some of the accountable talk strategies they already know.

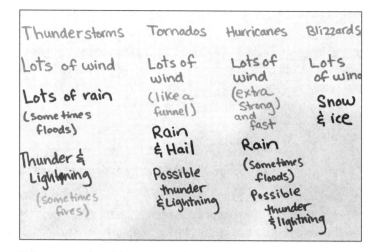

FIG. 19–3   A chart about storms based on the read-aloud book, *Super Storms*

In the last unit, you may have worked on a few ways to engage students in responding to the text and to one another. Draw on this learning and on charts from that unit, such as the "Readers Talk about Books" chart developed in the Unit 1 *Building Good Reading Habits* read-aloud.

If students need help launching the discussion, you might put forth a question or a statement that could help them build a conversation, such as, "What is important to know about super storms?"

Some students may need help listening to and building upon one another's ideas. If so, teaching them the phrases "One example is . . ." and "What do you mean?" can work wonders in helping them to listen more carefully and to talk in more connected ways. This is crucial because adding examples onto one another's statements helps students to link ideas and to process the information they are learning. Also, clarifying the text and each other's comments reinforces the idea that students should be seeking to understand information and listening in such a way as to help them learn more and become smarter about the topic.

As students talk about the book, project parts related to what students are discussing using a document camera, if you have one available. In so doing, you can encourage students to refer to the text as they talk.

After your book talk, you might say to students, "Next time we read this book, we can reread the most important parts. Which parts should we talk *more* about? Which parts should we reread? Turn and tell your partners which three parts you think we should study next time."

BEFORE YOU READ

Mark selected parts of the book for rereading.

Today, we suggest you reread selected parts of the book to engage students in thinking more deeply about the topic of super storms. Rereading parts of the book will help students learn more, and it models what students should do when they read and reread their own books independently. Before you read, remind students which parts they selected during the previous read-aloud session to reread and think and talk more about. It may be that they chose to revisit and think more about thunderstorms, tornados, and hurricanes. Whichever parts they selected, have them marked with a Post-it, ready to be reread and thought about more extensively.

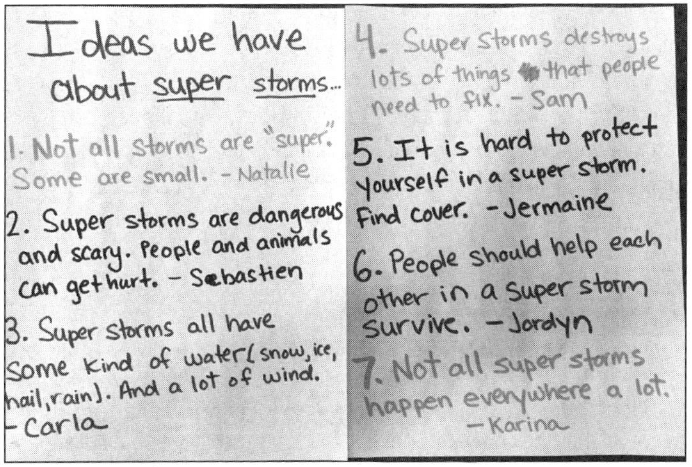

AS YOU READ

Recruit students to think more deeply about the text as you reread sections of it.

As you reread various parts of the book, you may ask students to listen to each part with a specific angle to think more deeply about. Choose an idea that the class generated and reread parts with that in mind. Perhaps you'll say, "As we read about thunderstorms, let's really think about reasons why they are *dangerous* super storms. Let's also study the pictures and think about what they are teaching us about super storms."

If you're rereading the pages about thunderstorms, take a few opportunities to invite students to turn and talk about how various pages or parts fit with an idea. Remind your students to use both the text and the pictures. For example, at the end of page 7, you might say, "So, how might this be dangerous?" At the end of page 11, you might show the photograph and say, "Look closely at this photograph. What do you notice? How does that fit with what the words say?"

As you move to another part of the book, such as the section about tornados, you may repeat some of the above prompts to give students more practice with them. At the end of pages 14 and 15, you might show students how a reader answers a previous question and then rereads with this new information in mind. You might say something like, "We know that tornados cause a lot of damage. Thunderstorms have lightning and a *lot* of rain. What makes tornados so dangerous? The wind. Let's reread these pages, thinking about the wind. Let's study the pictures and think about what happens."

In the third and final section you and your students have chosen to reread, you could channel them to practice some compare-and-contrast work. If you've decided to reread the section about hurricanes, you might say to your students, "As we read about hurricanes, let's think about why *they* are so powerful and dangerous. Let's think about how hurricanes are the same as other types of storms, like thunderstorms and tornados, and how they are different. As you

FIG. 19–4 A chart of ideas from the whole-class conversation about *Super Storms*

hear something that is the same as another kind of storm, put your thumb on your knee. I will stop and give everyone a chance to turn and talk about what they see that is the same."

After you give students a few opportunities to turn and talk, give them some examples of what it might sound like to talk about similarities between storm types. You might, for example, say, "Hurricanes have strong, fast winds, just like tornados." You also may decide to reread this portion of text, looking for ways to highlight the differences. You might start off rereading the section by saying, "Hurricanes, though, are the *most* powerful and deadliest. Let's figure out, not only what is the *same* about hurricanes and other super storms, but also what is different. Let's reread again, and this time, put your thumb up on your knee if you hear a difference."

AFTER YOU READ

Invite students to share important learning from the book in small groups.

At the end of rereading and talking about various sections of the text, give your students a last opportunity to talk about *all* that they now know about the topic they have studied, super storms. You might have your students make small groups in the meeting area to have a final chat about the book. Ask partnerships in row one and row three to turn to a partnership behind them. Then you might say, "For our final chat, let's discuss in our groups things about super storms that we think are most important to tell other people, like our friends and families."

After brief conversations in small groups, you might bring students back together for a quick symphony share. Ask your students to sit in a large circle. Then ask them to share the biggest, most important things that they would tell others about super storms. You may say to your students, "So, as I point to you and wave my magic finger, say what you think is most important about super storms for others to know! Here we go, get ready to share!"

SESSION 3: AFTER YOU READ

p. 30: Invite students to share important learning from the book in small groups.

"For our final chat, let's discuss in our groups things about _____. These are the things we think are most important to tell other people, like our friends and families."

Shared Reading
Learning about the World through Reading

Text Selections

> *Owls*, by Mary R. Dunn

> "Eagle Flight" and "Migration," by Georgia Heard
> (You could choose any poem or song about birds to read and reread with your
> students. We chose these poems from the book *Creatures of Earth, Sea, and Sky* by
> Georgia Heard.)

We chose *Owls*, by Mary R. Dunn, because both the words and the photographs in this nonfiction
book are highly engaging. We also wanted to choose a complex text that would be above the level
that *most* first-graders are reading independently. This way, they can be working in a grade-level,
complex text with scaffolds and supports. This text lends itself to rereading and closely studying a
topic—owls, in this case—because the content and the text offer quite a bit of richness to uncover
across a week. Further, the detailed language allows for in-depth word study.

We recommend doing this shared reading in the first bend of the unit so that the book will be familiar
when used as a demonstration text later in the second and third bends.

On this day, you'll introduce two poems and a book. Plan to project these texts with a document camera, if you have one, and be sure to enlarge the photographs and illustrations as well as the print. You'll reread the texts to increase familiarity, and also to draw attention to the information that readers are learning about the world, as well as to the words on the page and ways to solve them. Take the opportunity to reinforce habits that you taught in your previous unit of study: setting yourself up to read with a sneak peek, studying pictures, rereading with a smooth voice, and so on. Begin to draw awareness to what is different about nonfiction books from the ones students read in the last unit. You can point out text features and also begin to highlight and talk about domain-specific vocabulary.

Of course, shared reading of a new text also offers the opportunity to do some word-solving work using the strategy of guessing covered up words. Select a few words to cover, and lead students to practice using MSV (meaning, structure, and visual) information to help figure out what those words could be.

Sometimes, when reading nonfiction texts, children tend to read more slowly and less fluently. Be sure when you read this text aloud, that your voice is not only fluent, but sounds as engaging as possible. Encourage students to read along both the first and second time you read the book. Coach them to try to emulate what you do with your voice to make the reading both fluent and engaging.

WARM UP: "Eagle Flight" and "Migration," poems by Georgia Heard

Invite students to join a shared reading of two poems and think about what can be learned from them.

"Readers, to warm us up today in shared reading, I have two poems to read! Let's read them together twice and think about the question 'What do these poems teach us about birds?' Ready to read?

"Let's read the first title: 'Eagle Flight.' If you have an idea about what we will be learning, put your thumb on your knee. Turn and tell your partner what you think we are going to learn. Don't just say one word. Try to say a lot about what we might learn about that topic!

"Readers, we are going to get really smart about birds! This first poem is going to teach us about eagles and how they fly and move. Do some of you already know how eagles fly and move? Let's see if this poem gives us the same information and whether we can learn anything new."

Together, you'll read "Eagle Flight." You might point to the beginning of each line of text as the whole class reads in one voice, making sure to model smooth and expressive reading, just as kids learned to do in Unit 1.

"Let's read the poem a second time. This time, let's read it with more rhythm in our voices. Tap your knees as we read. Let's try to keep the beat."

DAY ONE FOCUS

- ✔ Rally your nonfiction readers to say, "We are going to learn and get smarter about *a lot* of topics in this unit! Let's use all that we learned from our last unit to read together and discover the world together!"
- ✔ Draw attention to text features.
- ✔ Read and reread with fluent, expressive, rhythmic voices.
- ✔ Talk about and learn new domain-specific vocabulary words.
- ✔ Remind students of some basic word-solving skills that they learned in the last unit.
- ✔ Work on using MSV cueing systems by playing "Guess the Covered Word" with selected words.
- ✔ Become familiar with several new texts.

Again, you'll read the text together, this time with rhythm. As you read, try to keep one eye on the kids, gauging their engagement levels. You might pause on a particular line that seems to drag and say, "Let's try that one more time—with rhythm!" when it seems like a sizable number of kids need the encouragement and extra reminder.

When you've finished reading, ask students to talk with their partners about what they learned. You might say, "Doesn't it sound good when we read with rhythm? Now turn and tell your partner what you learned about how eagles fly and move."

Then, do the same thing with the poem "Migration."

BOOK INTRODUCTION AND FIRST READING: *Owls*, Mary R. Dunn

Engage students in doing a sneak peek of the shared reading book, using the cover, the back, and the table of contents to predict what the book might be about.

"Readers, we have a new book to read together. The title is *Owls*, and the author is Mary R. Dunn. Let's read this book together so we can learn about another kind of bird—owls! I wonder what will be the same and what will be different from what we have already learned about eagles and some birds that migrate? I hope we will learn not only interesting things about owls, but also become even smarter about the topic—birds. Let's study the cover and say what we notice in the photograph. Turn and talk." Give students a moment to chat with partners and then share a few observations with the group.

"Now, let's read the back cover together to get ourselves ready to read the book. Let's start learning right now about owls."

> *Owls*
>
> *Hunting at night, owls watch for prey with large eyes. These hunters are adapted to life in the dark. Learn more about these feathered nocturnal animals in* Owls.

"I bet some of you heard some really important things about owls. Like they are hunting for prey. Prey is . . . If you know, put your thumb on your knee. Michael, tell us."

"It's like little animals that they eat," he replied.

"Like maybe a mouse or something? Yes. And did you see that big word, *nocturnal*?" I pointed to it. "Let's reread this one more time and think about this word.

"*Nocturnal* means things that are awake in the night! Now we know that owls are awake at night, *and* that they hunt for food, small animals that are their prey! Now, let's do a sneak peek *inside* the book.

"Oh, look, a table of contents page. This is going to tell us what kind of information we will learn about owls. Let's read it together and think, 'What will this book teach us about owls?'" We read through the table of contents and then thought about what each chapter *might* teach us. Then we previewed the pictures in the first chapter. "Let's get ready for Chapter 1. Read the heading with me. 'Night Hunters.' Let's look at the next few pictures and see what we might learn just by peeking. Yes, probably about how they fly and move, and where they live, because we see them in a tree and there is a map. Let's read this chapter together."

Recruit students to join a shared reading of the book.

Throughout the reading, as you read together, you may voice over things such as "nine pounds, four kilograms. That's not a lot. Think about it, you probably weigh around forty pounds. You are four times heavier!" or, "Look, now we have a list of owl prey: mice, lizards, and birds. Let's reread. The commas will help us read this list."

You may cover up a word like *gulp*. Ask kids, "What words would make sense here? Let's think about what is happening and try and think about a couple of words that might fit. *Eat, slurp, chew*. These are all good guesses that sound right and make sense with what is happening. Now let's look at *all* the parts of the word. /g/ul/p/. Say it with me. 'Gulp.' I guess they eat really quickly in one bite. Let's reread this page now." You might choose a few additional words to cover up and ask students to guess, such as *silently* on page 10 and *listen* on page 20. This is often referred to as a game called Guess the Covered Word.

Image Peter Schwarz/Shutterstock

Owls have gray-white or brown-orange feathers. Soft wing feathers help owls fly silently.

You might cover up the heading of one section and say to your class, "Uh-oh, the heading is covered up! It's your job to think about what this section is mostly about. When we are done reading it, let's give this chapter a heading or a title." You might do this, for example, with the chapter about growing up, which starts on page 16.

You may decide to save the glossary section for the second reading. This way you can focus on vocabulary, rereading, and using the glossary as a way to check what people say.

REREADING WITH A FOCUS

Choose a focus for a shared rereading of the book, such as vocabulary.

You may decide to reread the text and focus on the vocabulary in the book. You may reread from the beginning, and when kids come upon a vocabulary word, you can stop them and ask what they think it means. You may stop on page 4 to talk about *nocturnal*, page 12 to talk about *talons*, and page 16 to talk about *hatch*." You might say, "Let's stop here and talk about what *nocturnal* means. I'll leave the book up so you can use the words and the pictures to help you talk about what it is *and* what it is *not*! I heard many of you say that it's when animals are awake in the night doing stuff and sleeping in the day. Let's check the glossary in the back and see what it says."

You also might say to kids while showing page 12, "Let's read this page and think about the question 'Is there a word here that we should talk about? A word that is important to owls *and* that might be kind of new to us?' *Keen*! That's a good word. *Talons*. Another great one! Let's reread, thinking about what these words mean, and then we will check for them in the glossary."

AFTER READING

After two readings, ask students to think about what they learned from the book.

When you have finished rereading *Owls*, say your students, "Now, let's try to remember all the things that we learned about *these* kinds of birds! Take out your fingers and see how many things you can list about owls! Turn and talk."

After giving students a chance to talk with their partners about what they learned, you might say, "Readers, you just sounded *so* smart talking about what you now know about owls. We are going to reread this book tomorrow and the next day, too. We are going to become stronger readers who know a *lot* about birds. Do you know what they call people who study birds? Orinthologists. We are studying birds, so we are like orinthologists!"

DAY TWO: Cross-Checking (MSV)

On this day, you can reread one of the poems and the book *Owls* with a focus on cross-checking words using all three sources of information: meaning, structure, and visual. Focus on working with your students to use all three sources of information to help them solve words as they are reading. Emphasize with your students the importance of reading with accuracy and checking to confirm what they read using meaning, structure, and visual information.

As readers move to level H, coach them to continue correcting themselves at the point of error. Reinforce reading multisyllabic words while thinking about what would make sense and sound right. Remind students to attempt reading words a few times and to be flexible and strategic when thinking about the words in their texts.

WARM UP: "Migration," Georgia Heard

Reread a poem together, emphasizing strategies for increasing fluency and expression.

Reread the poem "Migration," by Georgia Heard, to warm up and start the session off. You might ask your students, as they read, to create a beat by tapping their knees or snapping their fingers. Help children read with better phrasing and fluency by following the rhythm of the text.

Because it's a short poem, you may return to it, considering what sorts of gestures you could add to your reading to show the important things in the poem. Kids might make flapping motions, turn their arms into suns, or make their fingers blink like stars lighting up.

These two strategies will help to build more engagement, fluency, and understanding of what the poem is about.

SECOND READING: *Owls*, Mary R. Dunn

Remind readers to continue using all they know to solve words and to check that they are reading with accuracy.

Read *Owls* again, complimenting the hard work children did previously and telling them that today, those tricky words will be a bit easier, but that you'll still find places in the text where you'll need to ensure they're reading the words correctly. Use the prompts "Does that makes sense, sound right, and look right?" as you did yesterday.

You may decide to cover up a few key words and prompt students first to use meaning and syntax to make a guess, and then to check the letters and parts of the word to confirm. For example, you may cover up the word *through* on page 4. Ask students to reread this page and think what would sound right and make sense. Have students generate several possibilities. Then reveal the first two letters and then the whole word. You may discuss the silent *gh* at the end and the *ou*, making the long /u/ sound. This word may be one of your high-frequency word wall words that you have been practicing. If not, you may decide to add it now.

✔ Develop more fluency and expression.

✔ Orchestrate the use of multiple sources of information to solve words (meaning, syntax, and visual).

✔ Cross-check one source with another, asking, "Does it make sense? Does it sound right? Does it look right?"

✔ Practice breaking words apart and crashing the parts together while thinking about what would make sense and sound right.

✔ Identify keywords and use new vocabulary in discussing the text.

✔ Read for comprehension.

Night Hunters

Most owls sleep all day.
These nocturnal birds
wing their way through
the night sky.

Choose several words that you will feature, either highlighted with highlighter tape or circled with Wikki Stix™. You might pick a word such as *weigh*, *feathers*, or *silently*. As you read these pages, you might, for example, prompt kids to explain how they know that the word is *weigh*. What information can they use to confirm that is the word? They can certainly use the meaning of the text in this part, because it is about the size of owls. It also sounds fine grammatically. The letters are a little less helpful in this case. Again, the letters *gh* are silent at the end. You might discuss the unusual vowel pattern, reinforcing the strategy of trying out various sounds for vowels to find a word that sounds right and makes sense.

As you are rereading the text, pick some words for a *slow check*. As you read with your students, drop your voice out on purpose, so that you can listen for errors that students make. Whether they make an error or not, make sure that students are still cross-checking, using meaning and phonics. You might say, "Did that look right and make sense? Let's do a slow check!" Slide you pointer under the word, say each part slowly, and then put the word together and reread the sentence. Say to your students, "A slow check helps us make sure we're reading the words that are actually on the page. Let's keep reading!"

AFTER READING

Focus discussion after the reading on key words and what they mean.

At the end of your rereading of the text, you may decide to select several key words and invite students to talk about what they mean and to retell the information in the text using the words. Say to your students, "These new words in this book help us to understand key information about owls." Then display the words: *nocturnal*, *keen*, *silently*, *sharp*. "Let's first talk about what these key words mean. Let's take the first word and say what it is and what the opposite of the word is. Give an example to help you describe it." If students have a hard time, reread the portion of the text with the word, and then ask a couple of students to make suggestions.

Repeat this with each of the words and then say, "Let's retell some important information using these words." Students then can turn and talk to one another. Listen for how students discuss and describe how owls hunt for food. Coach students to use the key words in their talk. Then have a student or two share their responses with the whole class.

At the end, you might say to your students, "As we read our books, let's do the same thing! Try to really pay attention to the words on the page and what they mean. Really think about what the author is trying to teach us, so that we can get smarter and smarter about the world!"

DAY THREE: Word Study

On this day, focus on your word study work. You may select a few phonics features to work on, as well as a few high-frequency words. You may also decide to use this session to help students work on reading multisyllabic words. Help them crash words or break them into parts, all the while thinking about what word would make sense within the particular context.

Strengthening the work that students are doing in phonics and spelling through shared reading will give students more practice in context, and it will also provide them with more feedback on their reading.

WARM UP: "Eagle Flight" and "Migration," by Georgia Heard

Reread poems together with a focus on specific phonics features.

As you reread these two poems, select a few phonics features to study with your first-graders. You may decide, for example, help your students by inviting them to do a word hunt for long and/or short vowel sounds in words and do a quick sort with those words. Note that students cannot depend solely on the way words look, but will need to work on listening to how words sound.

You might say to your students, "Let's read 'Migration' again! This time, let's think about the words and which ones have long vowel sounds and which ones have short vowel sounds. I will keep track here on the white board, on this T-chart, so that we can sort them." Stop after the first stanza and say, "So, are there any long vowel sounds? Search and find! Are there any short vowel sounds? Search and find!"

You may want to study inflectional endings, such as *ing* or *ed*. As students are rereading "Eagle Flight," they will encounter five *ing* words. You might cover up the *ing* in each word. As students read that word, ask them to confirm the ending. Show them the two parts of each word. Then say to students, "If we wanted to say that the eagle glides, how would we write that word?" Work on building other endings to words, so that students understand how to both read and write words with various inflectional endings.

DAY THREE FOCUS

✔ Reread with fluency.

✔ Word study: high-frequency words

✔ Word study: choose several phonics features.

✔ Work on breaking up multisyllabic words.

THIRD READING: *Owls*, Mary R. Dunn

Continue relevant word work while rereading the book together.

As you reread *Owls*, you can continue to sort words with long and short vowel sounds. You can then sort words within the lists and discuss what is similar and different about the spellings of these words. You may decide, rather than rereading the whole book, to select a chapter or two to focus on rereading.

After you have read a section in *Owls*, you may decide to select a multisyllabic word (or two) to study and discuss. For example, after you read the section "Up Close!" you might select the word *kilograms*. You may use a white board and write words with your students, or you may decide to distribute white boards to your students. On your own white board, write the first part of the word *kilograms*, *kil*. You may say to your students, "Let's say the first part together: /kil/. Aha! See how the vowel is inside the consonants like that? That's a closed syllable. That's a short vowel pattern! Now I will add the next part: *o*." Write it on the white board. "Let's crash the two parts together and read it. Now let me write *gram*. Let's crash all the parts together and read it: /kilogram/." You can continue in this way, and then reread the page containing the word. Practicing this with a couple of words, looking closely at the word both in and out of context, will be helpful preparation for encountering longer words in text.

AFTER READING

Follow shared reading with additional transferable word work.

After your third reading, you might choose a few words to add to your word wall, such as *through* or *enough*. Select a couple of words and talk about what they look like and sound like. Then ask kids to come up with a chant of the letters. Make sure that the clusters of sounds are grouped together somehow in the chant. For example, kids might chant, "en-ou-ggggggggh! Enough!" Encourage them to think about ways to make it more memorable. Then cover up the word and ask students to write it. Next, uncover it and ask them to check it.

After you've done that with a few words, you can say, "I am going to add these to our word wall. I'm going to box off the *gh* in this word to remind us that sometimes it's silent, and other times it makes the /f/ sound. Let's see, where should we put *enough* in order with all the other *e* words?"

To end the session, you might say, "Remember that you can use what you learn about words for our word wall and what you learn during word study time to help you think about words that you are reading. Using what you know about how words look and sound can help you think about the words in your books and what the book is trying to teach you. Remember to use the letters and sounds, as well as thinking about what makes sense, to help you as you read all of your books!"

DAY FOUR: Fluency and Expression

WARM UP: "Little Bird, Little Bird" (folk song)

Read and reread songs with related themes together, focusing on fluency and expression.

Singing songs is a wonderful way to build fluency and to develop a greater repertoire of texts. It can also demonstrate how information can be taught through various genres. Choose a song, perhaps about birds, to read and reread as your warm up. You might read it along with a recording or just sing it without accompaniment. You might pick a song like "Blackbird," by the Beatles, or "Three Little Birds," by Bob Marley. You might choose a folk song, such as "Little Bird, Little Bird," which Woodie Guthrie helped to popularize.

In any case, read and reread the song, working with students on first understanding the phrasing, how words are grouped together in the song. After you have read the song once, make sure you take the opportunity to quickly retell what the song is about. Then proceed with a few consecutive rereadings.

You may reread the song with your students, thinking together about where your voices might place some extra emphasis in the song. Finally, reread it once more, thinking about the expression of your voices, gestures that would be fun to accompany the singing, and ways to show expressions on your faces.

FOURTH READING: *Owls*, Mary R. Dunn

Reread the book together once again, emphasizing fluency and expression.

On this day, emphasize reading and rereading with a fluent voice. You might talk to your students about how it is important to use a voice that is smooth and interesting to listen to, even as nonfiction readers. While many of their nonfiction books are not stories, you might draw an analogy to people in the world that read informational texts out loud. News reporters, documentary narrators, radio show hosts, and TV personalities such as the Kratt brothers (from the PBS show *Wild Kratts*) are all types of people who use their voices to make informational texts come alive and sound interesting and important.

You may say to your students, "When you read out loud or even in your head, try to get the sound of the text in your mind! Rereading can help you figure out how it sounds best and makes the most sense to you! Let's reread parts of *Owls* and try to get our best news reporter voices going!"

As students are rereading the text, you may decide to work on phrasing or reading with more expression, or you may decide to emphasize stress. Whatever you decide the focus to be, give kids a lot of practice with that skill. Also, help them think about why they are stressing, expressing, or phrasing the text the way that they are. Teach them to think

DAY FOUR FOCUS

✔ Read and reread new and familiar texts, emphasizing fluency and expression.

✔ Use shared writing to create an extension of a familiar text.

critically about how it sounds. Give kids a couple of options of how they might read selected portions to show them how one can think and rethink a section of text and the way it sounds.

For example, perhaps you might reread the section "Staying Safe." You might say, "Lets read that first sentence and think about what word we could emphasize with our voices." Then ask students, "Why might this be an important word to stress?" If students have a hard time thinking of a reason, you might supply one or two yourself. Then, when you read as a class, you can say, "Is there a different word we could try to emphasize?" Repeat this a couple of times with various sentences on the page. Giving students practice with adjusting their stress (or phrasing or expression) can help them think about how they are using their voices to convey the syntax and meaning of the text, thus making it easier to understand and remember the information that they read.

AFTER READING

Follow up shared reading with shared writing to extend the text.

You may decide at the end of your shared reading experience today to do some shared writing. You might select two sections where you studied fluency today and ask students to write more text about that subject. You can create a short text extension that can be reread through shared reading later.

You might say to your students, "Let's see what else we can say about the two sections that we read. Let's start by thinking about the section 'Staying Safe.' What else could we say about this topic? What else could we teach in this section?" Students may say things such as "Owls stay safe by flying away. If they hear something, like a cat or a bird near them, they fly off the tree as fast as they can. Then they look for another place to perch." Whatever students come up with, they can practice articulating the sentences, and you can write them down where everyone can see. Every few words, have students reread the writing with their best fluent voices. In the end, you'll have a longer, more elaborated informational book.

DAY FIVE: Putting It All Together

WARM UP: "Eagle Flight" and "Migration," by Georgia Heard

Quickly reread the familiar poems to build confidence, excitement, and fluency.

You might start by rereading the two poems you have been reading all week, reviewing the many things that you have taught. You may say to your students, "Now that we know these poems so well, let's use our best voices to reread them another time, sounding like the bird experts that we have become!"

DAY FIVE FOCUS

✔ Reread different types of familiar texts (poems, songs, books) with fluency and expression.

✔ Orchestrate all three cueing systems while reading, and use everything learned all week.

✔ Demonstrate new content learning in discussions about the text.

✔ Generate questions and topics for further reading and study.

Read the poems together in unison. Listen for whether kids bring a rhythm to their reading to create more fluency. You might say to your readers, "Our voices not only sound like experts, but they sound like music. Let's reread one more time, paying attention not only to the rhyme and the line breaks, but also to the punctuation."

At the end of your reading, ask your students to turn and tell all that they have learned about birds from these two poems. Suggest that they make a list across their hands and then share their newfound expertise.

FINAL READING: *Owls*, Mary R. Dunn

Emphasize how using all three sources of information (MSV) while reading, along with rereading, can make the reading so much stronger.

As you reread *Owls* for the final time this week, listen to how students' fluency has improved. Listen to the tempo and consider whether kids are reading smoothly at a regular pace. Do not slow down for them to keep up. Instead, see if students' voices keep up with yours. As they do, soften your voice so that their voices become the prominent sound in the room.

You might have a word covered in a couple of different parts to create some challenging spots for them as readers. Encourage your students to use MSV to help solve these words on the run. Throughout the reading, you may pause a few times to invite students to retell what a section was about, using some of the key words in the text as they talk.

AFTER READING

Celebrate the fun you have had reading this book over and over again.

You may want to have a book talk about what you all have learned about owls and birds in general. You might pose a question such as "What are the most important things that people should know about owls, and why?" Encourage students to name facts they have learned and also to think about why they might be important and what they might teach about other birds.

At the end of the book talk, you may want to say to your students, "Now that we know so much about eagles and how they fly, migration, and owls, what else do we want to know about birds? Specifically, what would we like to investigate to find out if what we already know is true about other birds?" You can field several types of questions; some may be follow-up questions from the texts you have read, some may be inquiries into ideas students now have about birds, and others may seem random.

Throughout the month, you can read about a variety of topics with your students through shared reading. However, you may want to select a couple more texts about birds to show students how to pursue topics of interest.